Mel Bay's Modern

GUITAR METHOD GRADE 4

Expanded Edition

Online Audio www.melbay.com/93203EEB

AUDIO CONTENTS

Audio 1

1 Etude in E Major
2 E Scale Studies Ex. 1
3 E Scale Studies Ex. 2
4 E Scale Studies Ex. 3
5 E Scale Studies Ex. 4
6 E Scale Studies Ex. 5
7 E Scale Studies Ex. 6
8 Prairie Sunset
9 Epigram
10 Picking Studies Ex. 1
11 Picking Studies Ex. 2
12 Picking Studies-C Picking
13 Picking Studies-G Picking
14 Picking Studies-D Picking
15 Picking Studies-A Picking
16 Picking Studies-E Picking
17 Fourth-Position Etude #1
18 Etude #2
19 Starburst
20 Eclipse
21 I Gave My Love a Cherry
22 Cheyenne Wells-4th Pos.
23 Study #3-4th Pos.
24 Waltz
25 Italian Air (Multi-Pos. Study)
26 A Triplet Etude
27 A Study #2-4th Pos.
28 Fourth-Position Etude
29 A Study #3-4th Pos.
30 Stuck in the Kitchen-4th Pos.
31 Exhilaration-4th Pos.
32 Rose O Sharon-4th Pos.
33 Morning Dance-4th Pos.
34 A Scale Study #4-4th Pos.
35 Key of A Review
36 C♯ Minor Studies-4th Pos. Ex. 1
37 C♯ Minor Studies-4th Pos. Ex. 2
38 C♯ Minor Studies-4th Pos. Ex. 3
39 C♯ Minor Studies-4th Pos. Ex. 4
40 C♯ Minor Studies-4th Pos. Ex. 5
41 Bering Sea-4th Pos.
42 Portrait-4th Pos.
43 Nocturne-4th Pos.
44 Images-4th Pos.
45 Reflection-4th Pos.
46 Sarabande (Duet in C♯ Minor)
47 Ivy Leaf Reel
48 Little House Round the Corner
49 Minueto
50 Lyric Moment-4th Pos.
51 Daydreams-4th Pos.
52 Star of Bethlehem-4th Pos.
53 Schooner-4th Pos.
54 St. Clair's Hornpipe-4th Pos.
55 Fifth-Position Etude #1
56 Fifth-Position Etude #2
57 The Court Jester (Fifth Position)
58 Woodlands-5th Pos.
59 Narcissus-5th Pos.
60 Sonatina in F Major-5th Pos.
61 The Commentator
62 Fifth-Position Etude #3
63 Stallion at Daybreak-5th Pos.
64 Riley McGurk-5th Pos.
65 Levelland by Night-5th Pos.
66 Jonquil-5th Pos.
67 Sundance-5th Pos.
68 Clare Waltz-5th Pos.
69 High Five-5th Pos.
70 Traverse Bay-5th Pos.
71 Shadows
72 Ballad-5th Pos.
73 River Glen-5th Pos.
74 Sailors Hornpipe-5th Pos.
75 Meramec Echoes-5th Pos.
76 Buena Vista-5th Pos.
77 Suffolk-5th Pos.
78 Shamrock-5th Pos.
79 Ruby-5th Pos.

Audio 2

1 Key of Am-5th Pos. Ex. 1
2 Key of Am-5th Pos. Ex. 2
3 Key of Am-5th Pos. Ex. 3
4 Leipzig - 5th Pos.
5 J.S.-5th Pos.
6 Dance-5th Pos.
7 Silouette-5th Pos.
8 Starling-5th Pos.
9 Mirage-5th Pos.
10 B♭ Scale Etude
11 B♭ Studies-5th Pos.
12 Song-5th Pos.
13 Exploration-5th Pos.
14 Etude-5th Pos.
15 Minuetto
16 Triplet Etude in the Fifth Pos. #1
17 Triplet Etude in the Fifth Pos. #2
18 DeSoto-5th Pos.
19 Dora's Waltz-5th Pos.
20 Erin's Waltz-5th Pos.
21 Cross Country-5th Pos.
22 Snapshop-5th Pos.
23 Poem
24 Seventh-Position Etude
25 Waterfall-7th Pos.
26 Joplin-7th Pos.
27 Kreutzer's Etude-7th Pos.
28 Seventh-Pos. Etude in G
29 Sor's Song-7th Pos.
30 Breathe on me, Breath of God
31 Lucky Seven-7th Pos.
32 Rondo
33 Scale Study-7th Pos.
34 Gardenia-7th Pos.
35 Gypsy Rondo-7th Pos.
36 Portrait-7th Pos.
37 Discovery-7th Pos.
38 Dawn-7th Pos.
39 Passage-7th Pos.
40 Misty Night-7th Pos.
41 Sierra-7th Pos.
42 Vista-7th Pos.
43 Workout-7th Pos.
44 Glasgow-7th Pos.
45 Sunset-7th Pos.
46 Autumn-7th Pos.
47 Nightfall-7th Pos.
48 Cruising-7th Pos.
49 Muse-7th Pos.
50 Snowfall-7th Pos.
51 Panorama-7th Pos.
52 Natasha-7th Pos.
53 Farewell-7th Pos.
54 Ninth-Position Etude #1
55 Ninth-Position Etude #2
56 The Ninth Inning-9th Pos.
57 Maze-9th Pos.
58 Susan Lynn - Multiple Pos.
59 The Golden Wedding (La Cinquantaine)
60 Carcassi's Etude (A Major)
61 Norwegian Dance
62 Excursion (A Position Review)

WWW.MELBAY.COM

The Key of E Major

The key of E has four sharps. All F, C, G, and D notes are sharped.

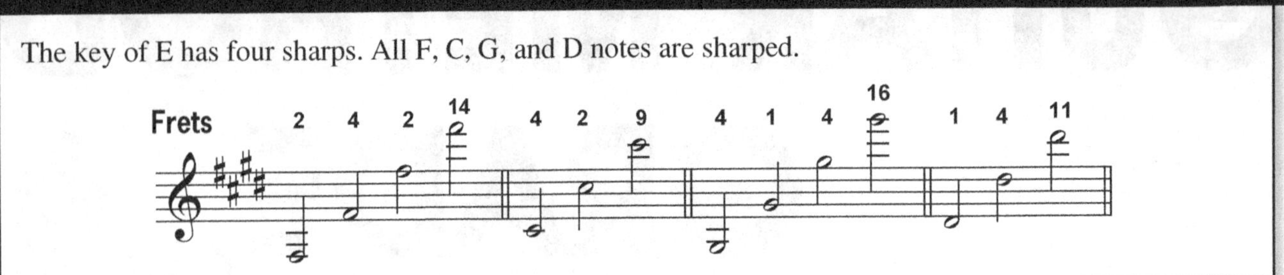

The E Major Scale

(Three Octaves)

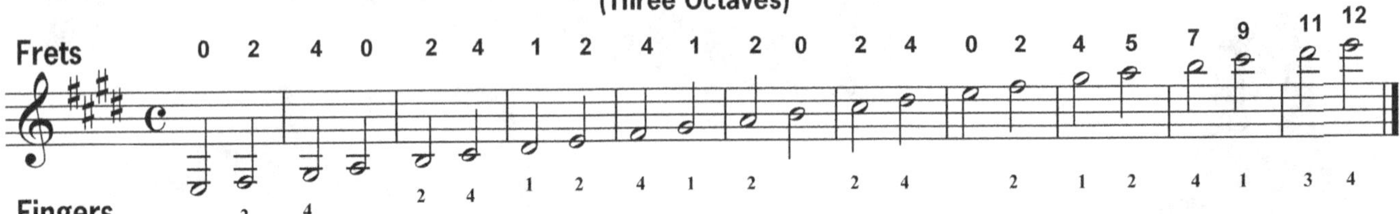

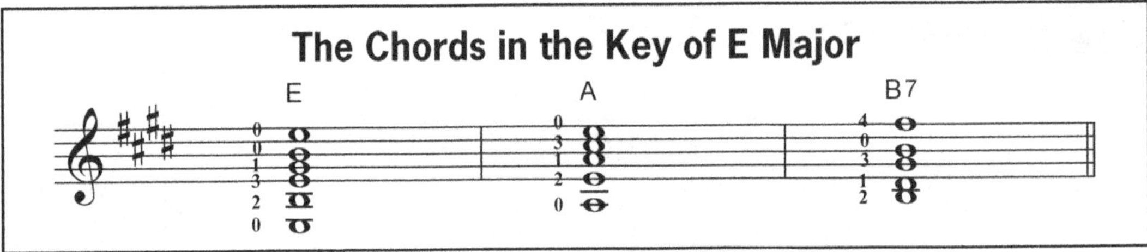

Etude in E Major

Mel Bay

Allegro

E Scale Studies

①

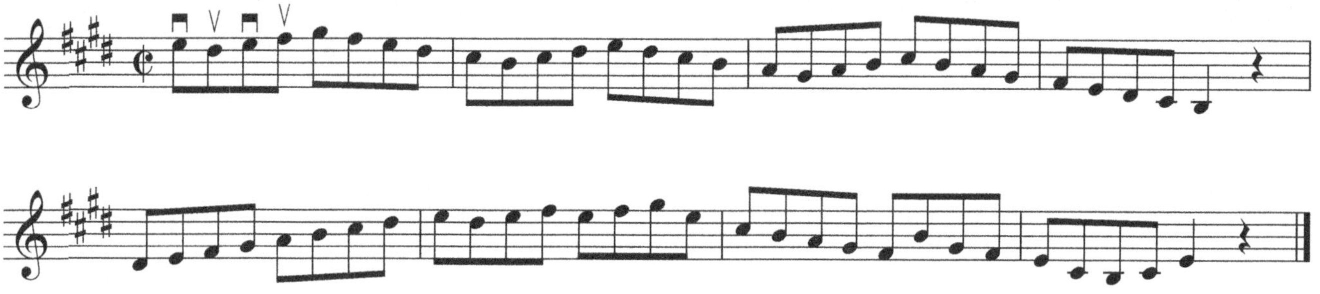

②

TRACK
3

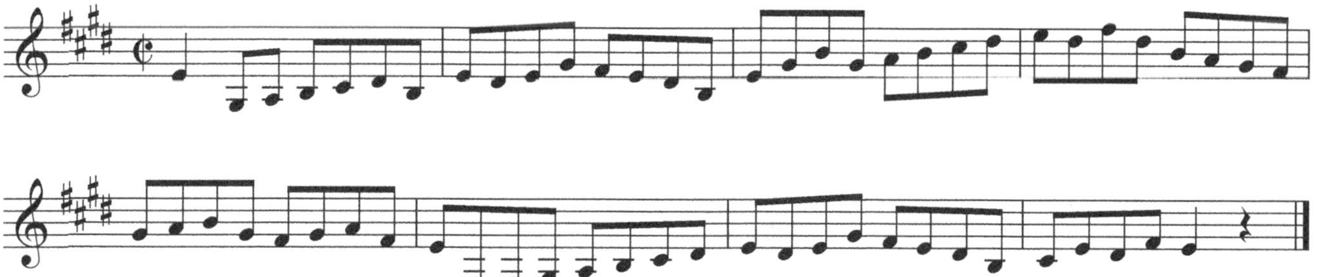

③

TRACK
4

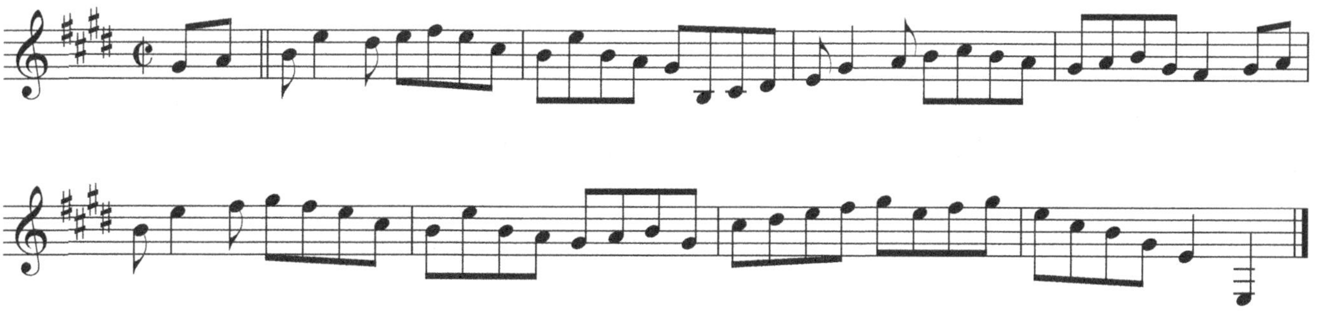

④

TRACK
5

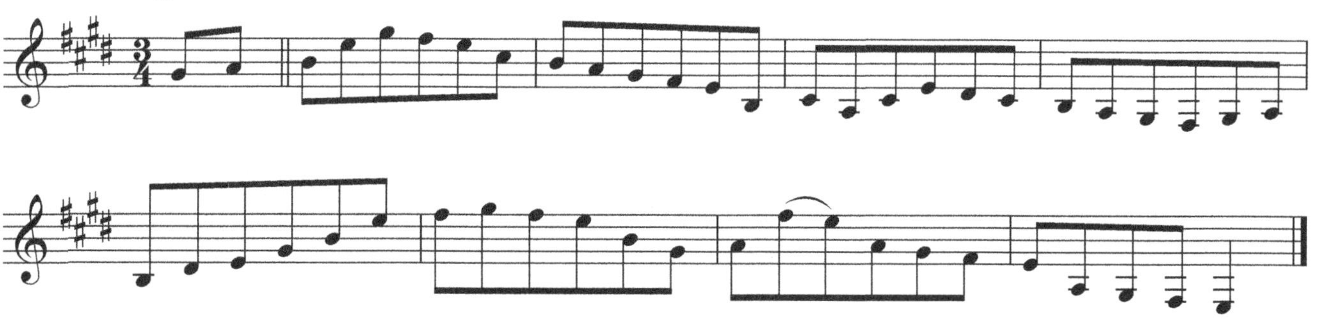

⑤
TRACK
6
⑥
TRACK
7
Prairie Sunset
TRACK
8
Medium tempo
E
A
E
A
WB
E
B7
E
A
E
A
E
A
E
B7
A
E

Epigram

TRACK 9

Picking Studies

TRACK 10

TRACK 11

Picking Studies
TRACK 12
C Picking
G Picking
TRACK 13
D Picking
TRACK 14
A Picking
TRACK 15
E Picking
TRACK 16

The Fourth Position

Starburst

Eclipse

I Gave My Love a Cherry
TRACK 21
Slowly
Ballad
ritard
Cheyenne Wells – 4th Pos.
TRACK 22
E B7 A E A E B7
E B7 A E A E B7 E B7 E
Fine
C♯m E C♯m B7 C♯m E C♯m B7
C♯m F♯m E B7 E
D.C. al Fine
Study #3 – 4th Pos.
TRACK 23

Waltz

TRACK 24

With the exception of the open B note, designated by the zero (0), the entire selection is in the 4th position.

Italian Air (Multi-Position Study)

TRACK 25

Guitar Solo

Matteo Carcassi
Arr. by Mel Bay

A in Fourth Position

Key of A

A Scale – 4th Position

A Arpeggio – 4th Position

A Triplet Etude

A Study #2 – 4th Position

Fourth-Position Etude
TRACK 28
Allegro
A Study #3 – 4th Position
TRACK 29
Andante
Fine
D.C. al Fine

Stuck in the Kitchen – 4th Position

Exhilaration – 4th Position

Rose O Sharon – 4th Position
TRACK 32
Moderately
W. B.
Fine
D.C. al Fine
rit.
Morning Dance – 4th Position
TRACK 33
Allegro
W. B.
Fine
D.C. al Fine

A Scale Study #4 – 4th Position

Key of A Review

TRACK 35

Slowly

Open Position

W. B.

4th Position

The Key of C Sharp Minor

(Relative to E Major)

The C sharp minor scales are played in the fourth position except where shown.

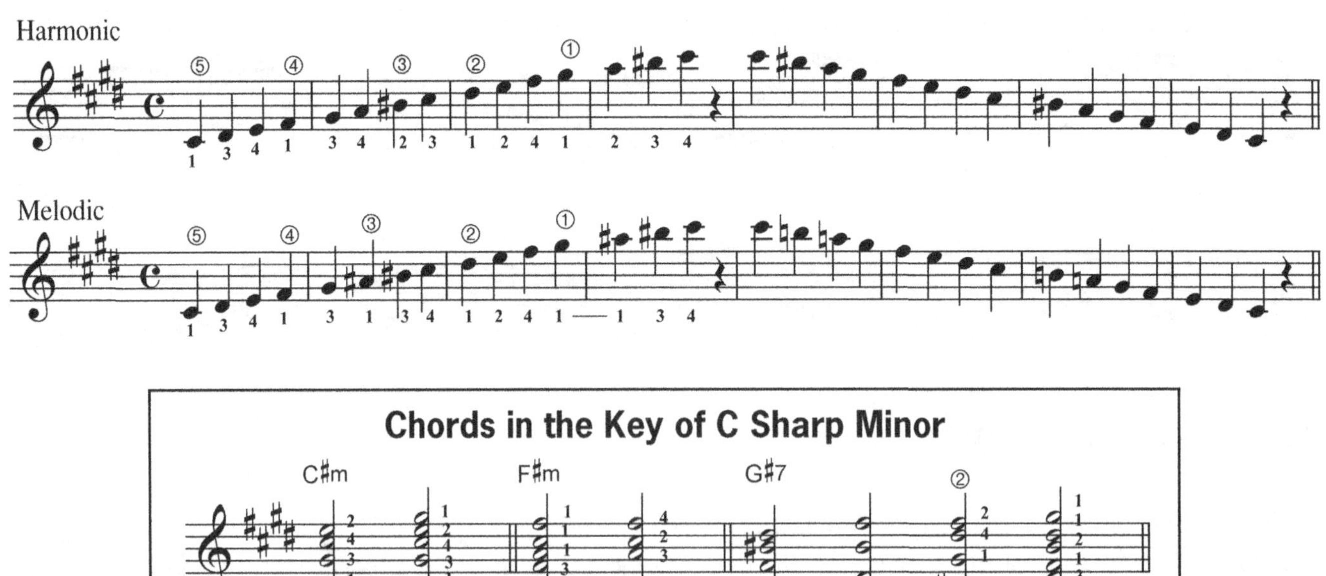

③
TRACK
38
1
⑤
④
TRACK
39
⑤
TRACK
40
Bering Sea – 4th Position
TRACK
41
Slowly
W. B.
3 2 1
③ ② ①

Portrait - 4th Position

TRACK 42

Slowly

W. B.

Nocturne - 4th Position

TRACK 43

Slowly

W. B.

Images – 4th Position

Largo

W. B.

3

③

Reflection – 4th Position

TRACK 45

Slowly

W. B.

1

③

Grace Notes

Grace notes are small notes which subtract their value from the note they precede. The technical term for the grace note is "appoggiatura." The grace note is crossed at the end and is played the same as slurs. When the grace note is on a different string from the principal note, pick it separately.

Ivy Leaf Reel
TRACK 47
D G Em A7 D
G Em A7 D
G D Bm A A7
D G D Em Bm A A7 D
Little House Round the Corner
TRACK 48
Irish Jig
D G A7
D A7 D
D A7 D A7 D A7 D A7
D A7 D A7 D A7 D

Minueto (from the Sonata Op. 25)

TRACK 49

F. Sor
Arr. by Mel Bay

Moderato

* Pick the first note and slur the remaining three

Key of D in Fourth Position

D Scale – 4th Position

D Arpeggio – 4th Position

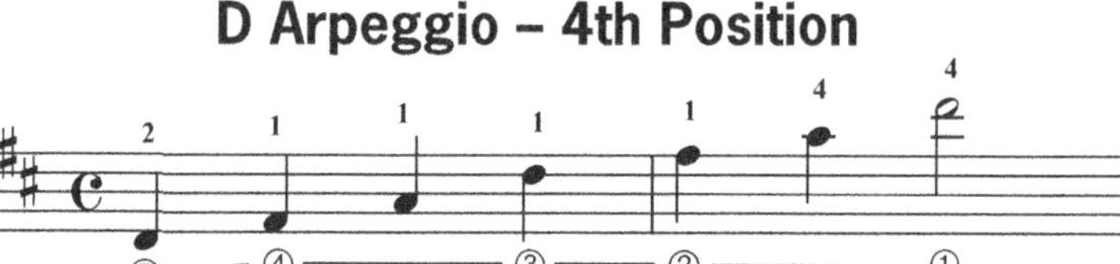

Lyric Moment – 4th Position

TRACK 50

Andante

W.B.

Daydreams – 4th Position

Slowly

W.B.

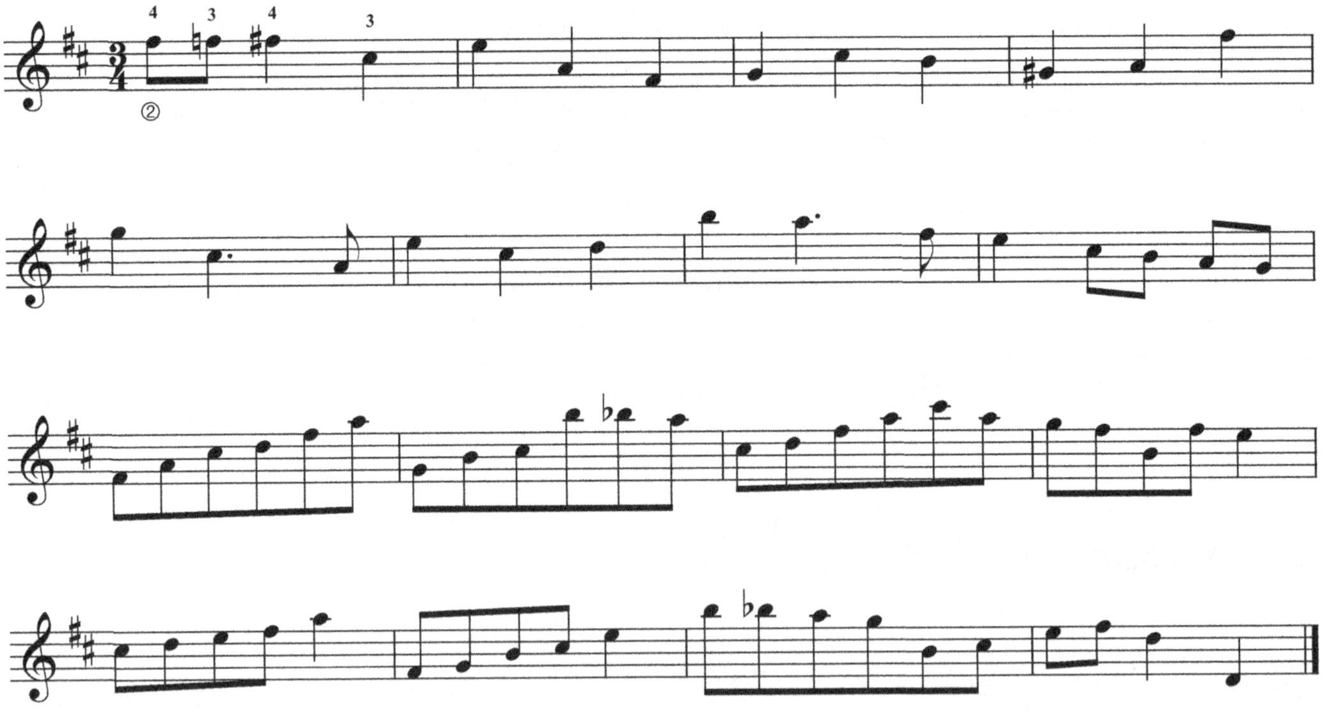

Star of Bethlehem – 4th Position

TRACK 52

Allegro

W.B.

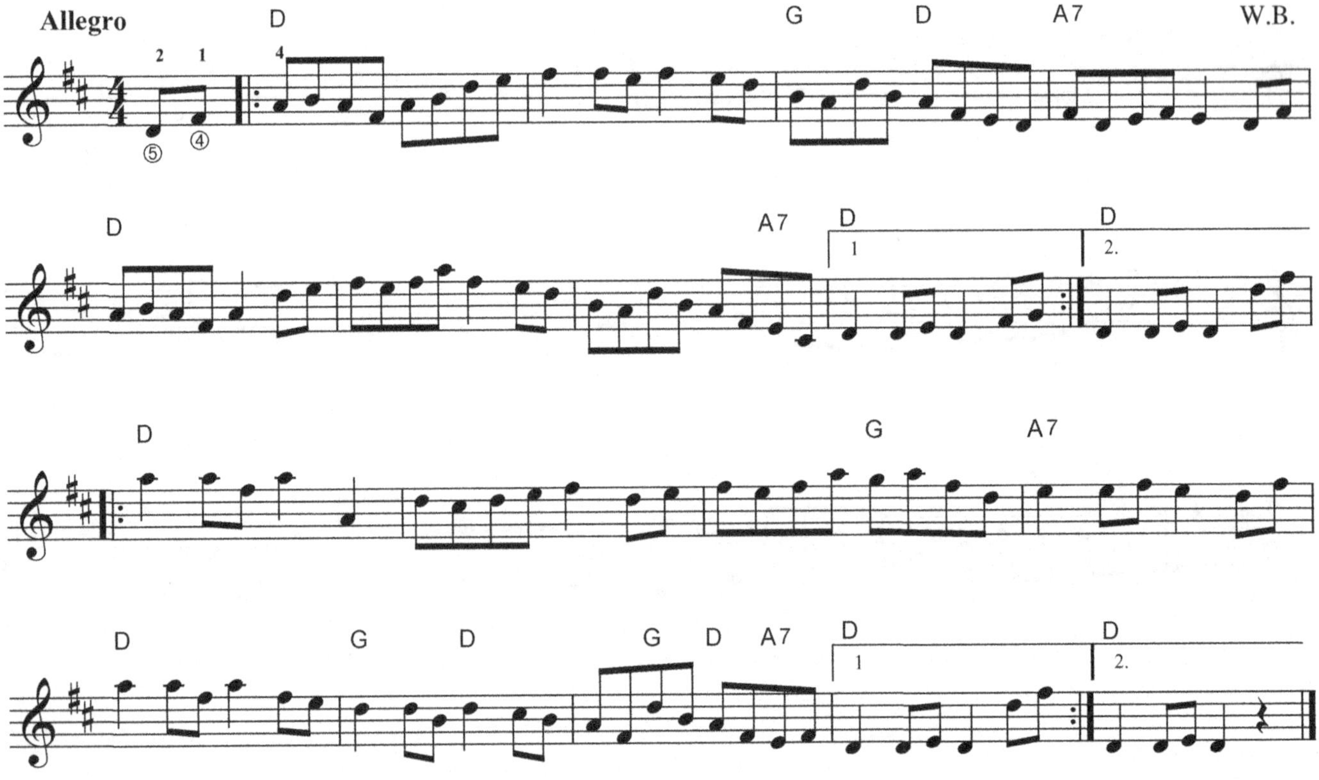

D G D A7

D A7 D D

D G A7

D G D G D A7 D D

Schooner – 4th Position 

Moderately

W.B.

Fine

2 1 2 4 3 1 1 - 1 3 - 1 3 - 3 1 3 4 2 (4) 3 (1) - 1 3

4 2 1 1 4 4

D.C. al Fine

St. Clair's Hornpipe – 4th Position

TRACK
54

4 2

D A G A7 D A7 D

A G A7 D A7 D

D G A7 D G A7

D G A7 D A7 D

The Major Chords

Three chord forms are used to produce the major chords. The forms are movable and should be practiced from the first to the tenth frets on the first four strings of the guitar. The forms are numbered I, III, and V, corresponding to the chord interval, namely root (I), third (III), and fifth (V).

The top note of the chords is on the first string. The top note of any chord will be the note highest in pitch. The top note of form I is the root of the chord. The top note of form III is the third, and the top note of form V is the fifth interval of the major chord.

Playing the forms chromatically up the fingerboard produces the following major chords:

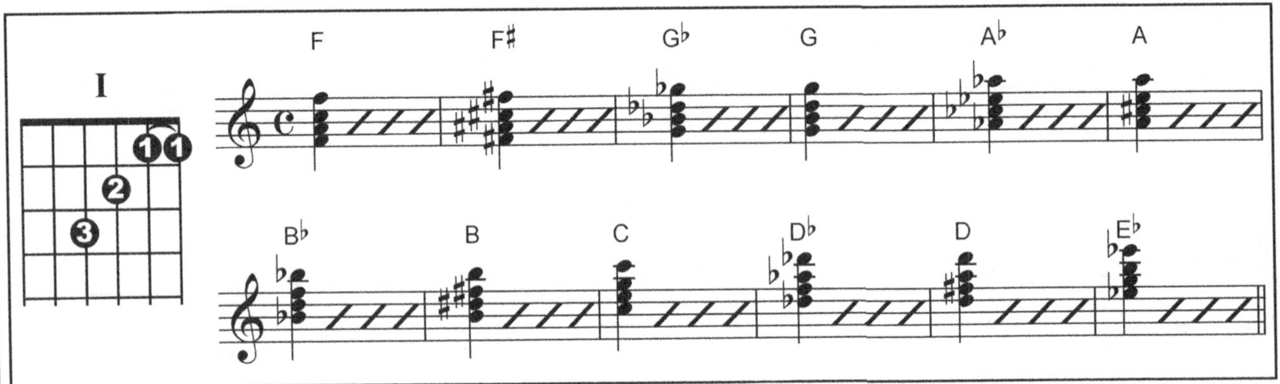

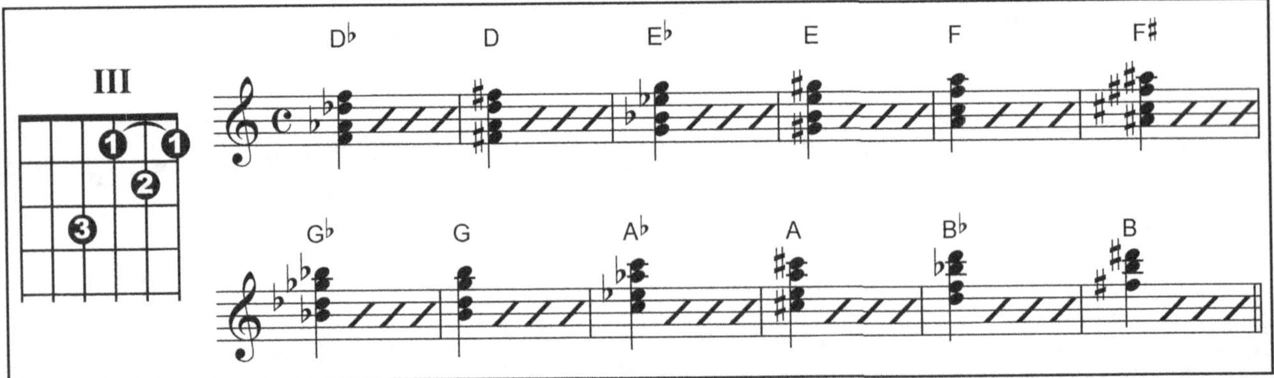

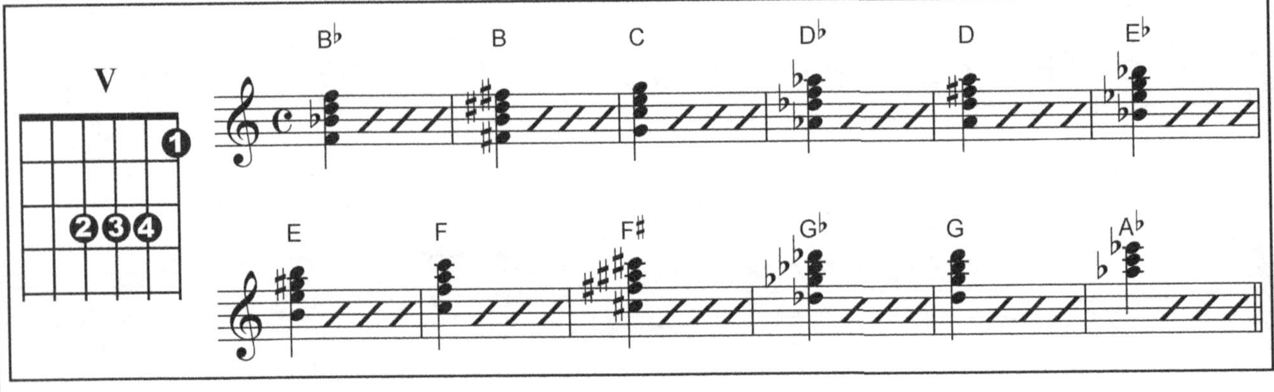

Note: This page should be memorized

The Fifth Position

Key of F

The Note-Spelling of the Major Chords

C (C-E-G) F (F-A-C) B♭ (B♭-D-F) E♭ (E♭-G-B♭) A♭ (A♭-C-E♭)
D♭ (D♭-F-A♭) G♭ (G♭-B♭-D♭) F♯ (F♯-A♯-C♯) B (B-D♯-F♯) E (E-G♯-B)
A (A-C♯-E) D (D-F♯-A) G (G-B-D)

Memorize

Fifth-Position Etude No. 2

Woodlands – 5th Position

Moderately

W.B.

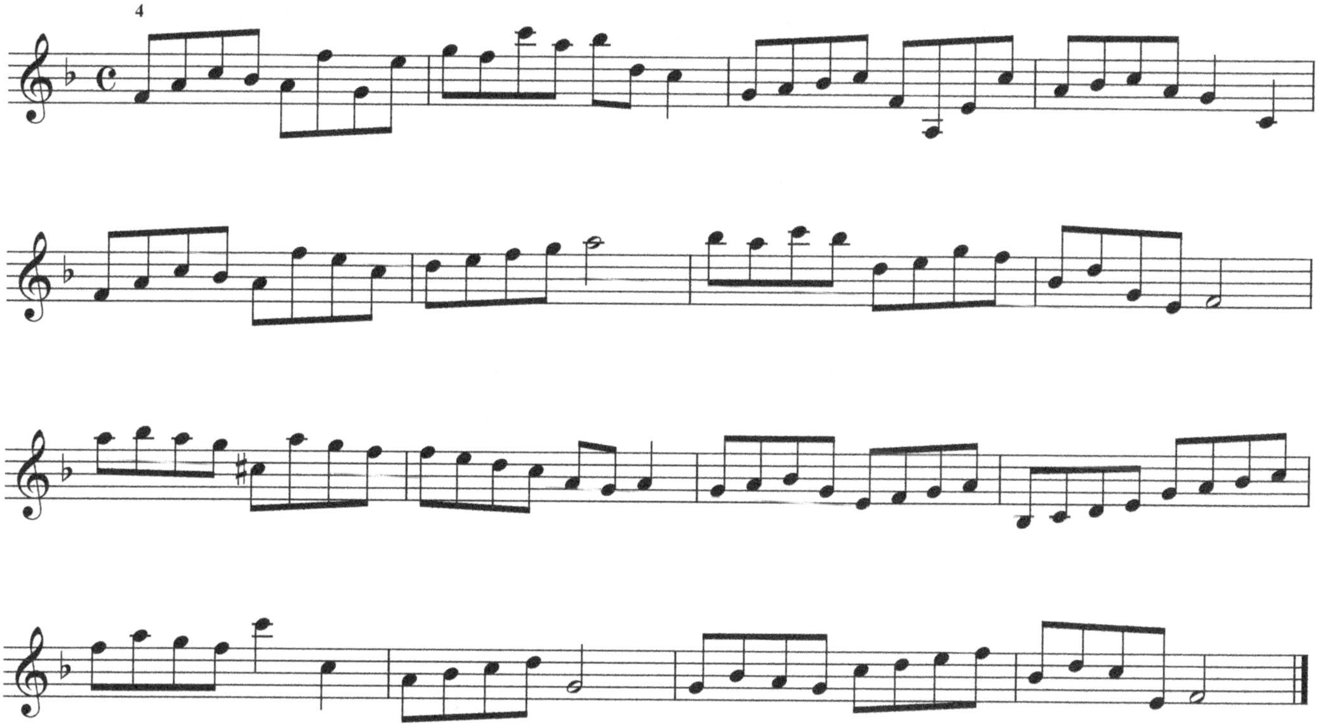

Narcissus – 5th Position

TRACK 59

Moderately

W.B.

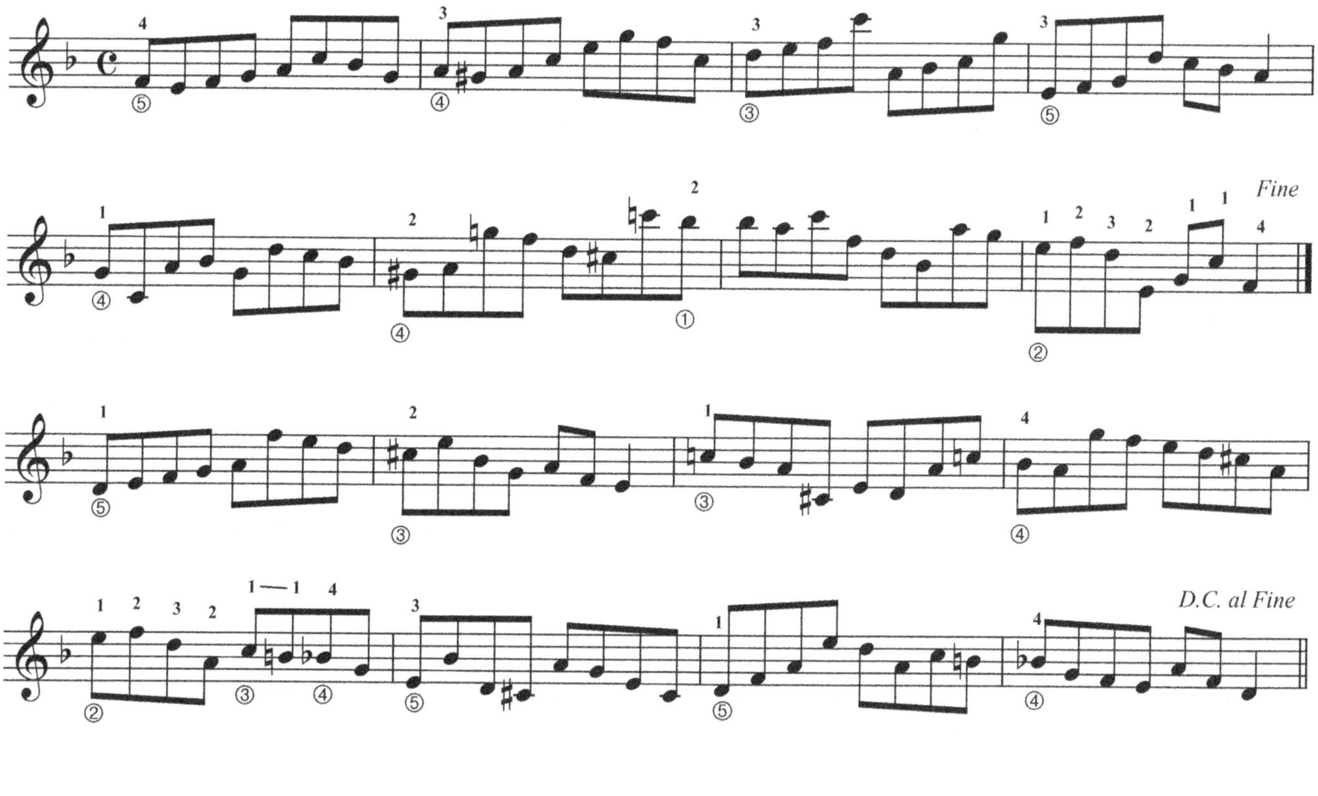

Fine

D.C. al Fine

Sonatina in F Major – 5th Position

Andante

The Commentator (Fifth Position)

Guitar Solo

Carcassi – Bay

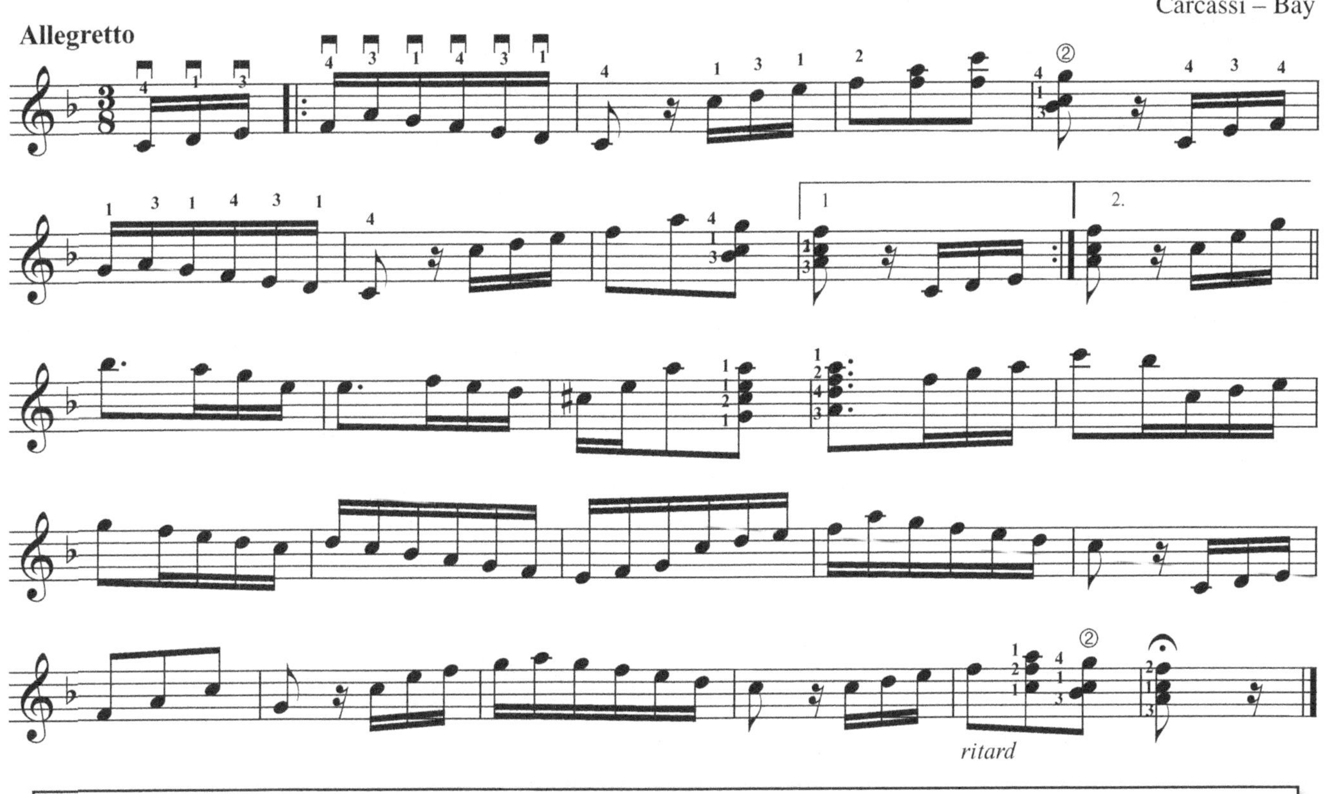

The Mixed Minor Scales

The **mixed** minor scale ascends in the **melodic mode** but descends in the **harmonic mode**.

Fifth-Position Etude #3

Stallion at Daybreak – 5th Position

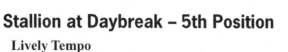

Lively Tempo

W.B.

F (1)—1 C7 F C7

F B♭ F B♭ C7 F *Fine*

F C7 F C7 F C7

F C7 F C7 C7 F *D.C. al Fine*

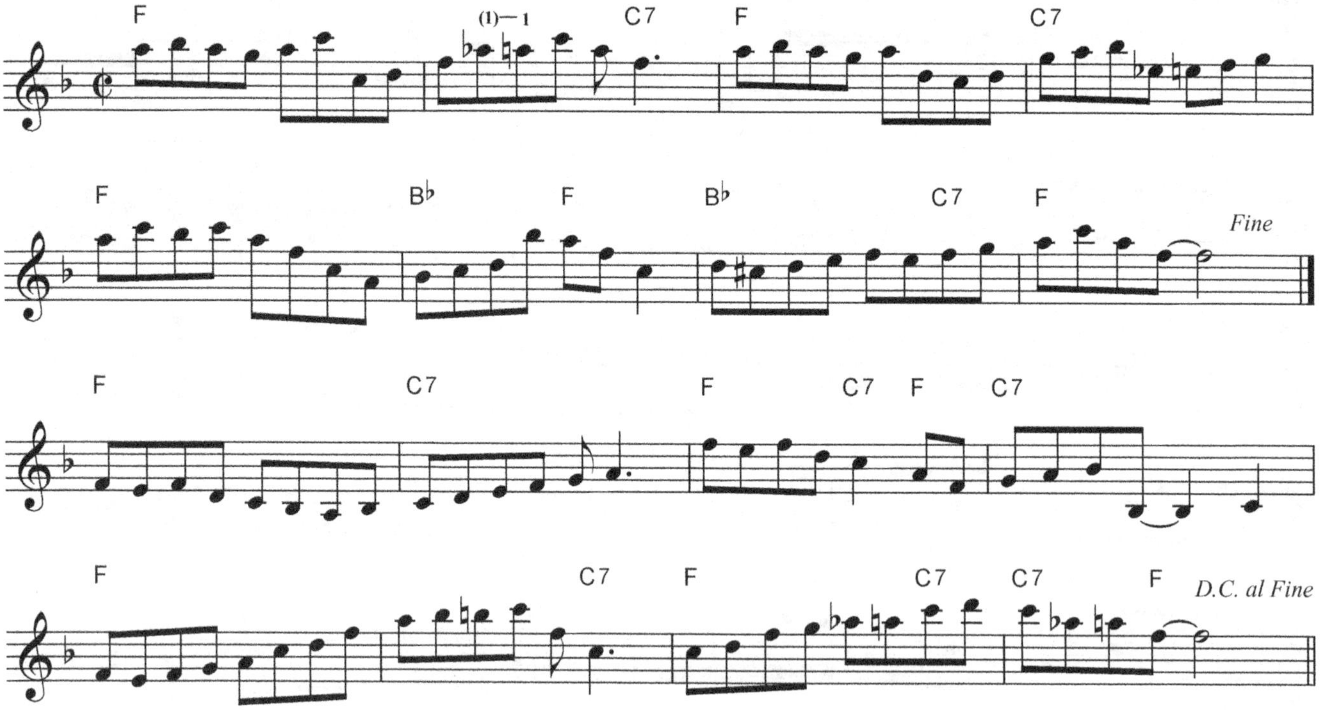

Riley McGurk – 5th Position

TRACK 64

Lively Tempo

W.B.

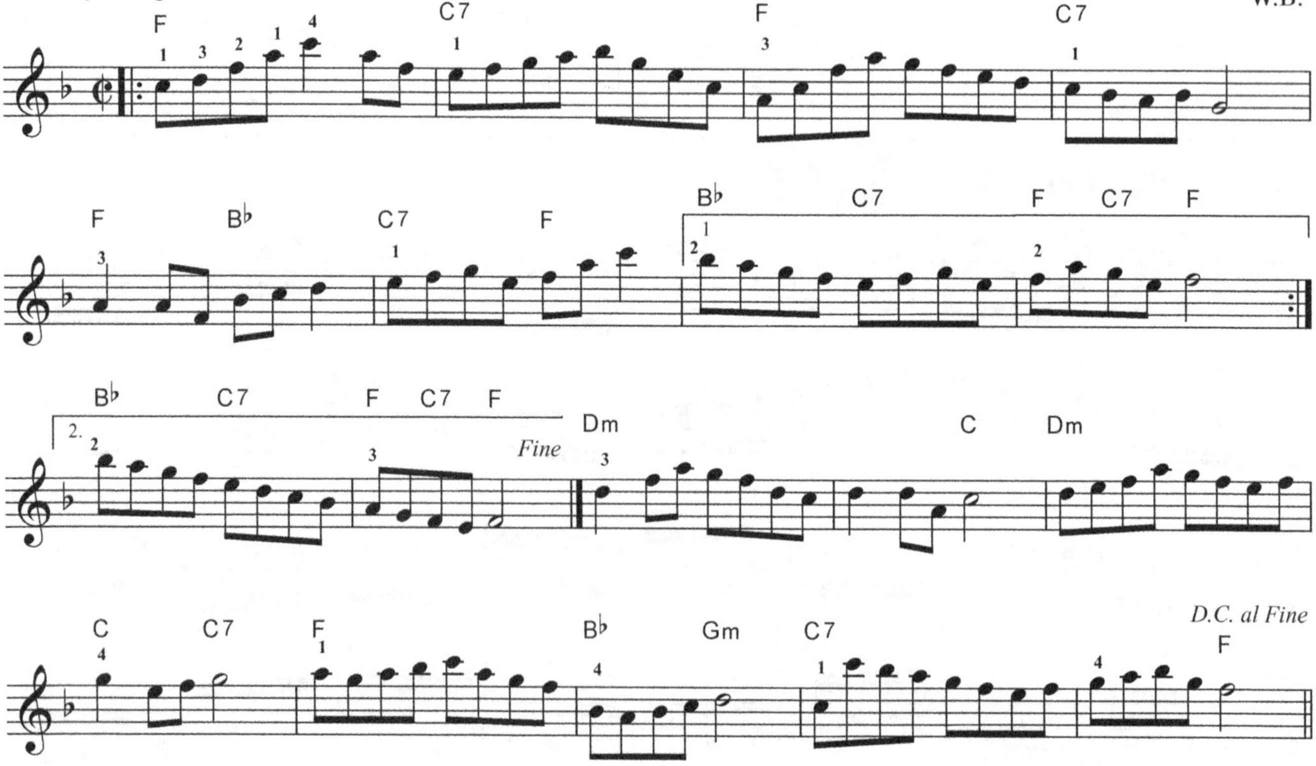

F C7 F C7

F B♭ C7 F B♭ C7 F C7 F

B♭ C7 F C7 F *Fine* Dm C Dm

C C7 F B♭ Gm C7 F *D.C. al Fine*

Dm Fifth Position

D Minor Scale / Harmonic Mode Scale – 5th Position
D Minor Arpeggio – 5th Position
Levelland by Night – 5th Position
TRACK 65
Dm
C
A7
Gm
Fine
D.C. al Fine
Jonquil – 5th Position
TRACK 66
Slowly
W.B.
Fine
D.C. al Fine

Sundance – 5th Position
TRACK 67
Slow Swing
W.B.
Dm
Gdim
A7
Dm
A7
Dm
A7(♯5)
Dm
A7
Dm
Fine
Gm
Dm
Gm
A7
Dm
D.C. al Fine
Gm
Gdim
A7
Dm
A7
Dm
A7(♯5)
Dm
Clare Waltz – 5th Position
TRACK 68
W.B.
Slowly
Fine
D.C. al Fine

High Five – 5th Position
TRACK 69
Swing Feeling
W.B.
Dm C Dm A7(♯5)
Dm Gm A7(♯5) A7 Dm
Fine
C Gdim Dm Gm A7 Dm Gdim A7
Dm A7(♯5) Dm A7(♭9) Dm
D.C. al Fine
Traverse Bay – 5th Position
TRACK 70
Medium Tempo
W.B.
Dm Gm Dm
A7 Dm A7 Dm Gm A7
Dm A7 Dm Dm A7 Dm Gm Dm Gm Dm
Fine
Gm Dm A7 Gm Dm
A7 Dm Gm A7 Dm
D.C. al Fine

Shadows

TRACK 71

Mazas – Bay

I
II
B♭
Dm
F dim
A7
B♭
Dm
F dim
A
Dm
Dm
Dm
Dm

Ballad – 5th Position

TRACK 72

Slowly

Divisee – Bay

River Glen – 5th Position

TRACK 73

Slowly

W.B.

Sailors Hornpipe – 5th Position
TRACK 74
Arr. by Mel Bay
Guitar Duet
I
II
F
C7
F
B♭
Gm7
C7
V Pos.
F
B♭
G7
C7
B♭
Gm7
C7
Major Chord Etude #2
C
F
B♭
E♭
A♭
D♭
G♭
F♯
B
E
A
D
G
C

Key of C – 5th Position

C Scale – 5th Position

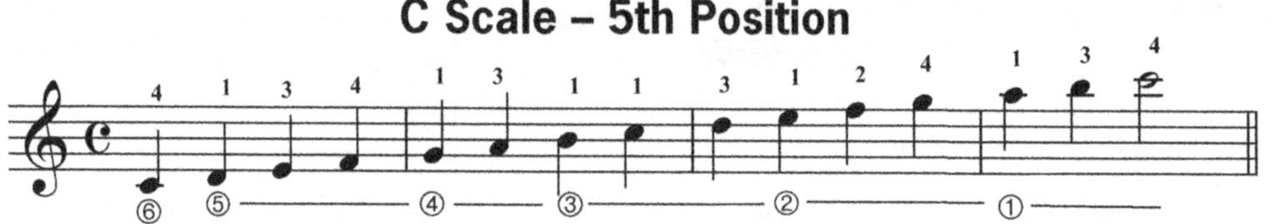

C Arpeggio – 5th Position

Meramec Echoes – 5th Position

TRACK 75

W.B.

Buena Vista – 5th Position

amrock – 5th Position
TRACK
78
Allegro
W.B.
Ruby – 5th Position
TRACK
79
Andante
W.B.

Key of Am – Fifth Position

A Minor Scale / Harmonic Mode Scale – 5th Position

A Minor Arpeggio – 5th Position

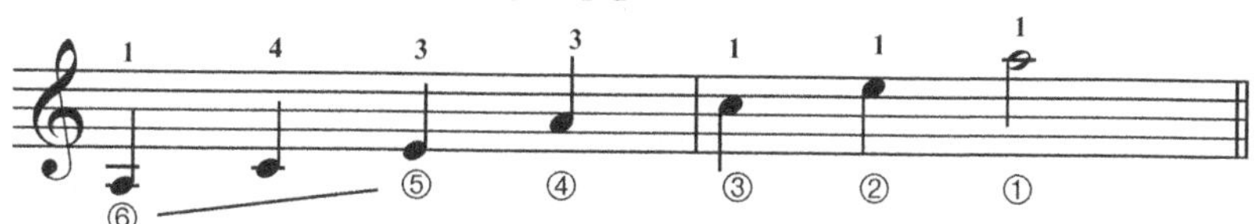

①

②

③

th Position
TRACK
4
W.B.
. – 5th Position
TRACK
5
Andante
W.B.

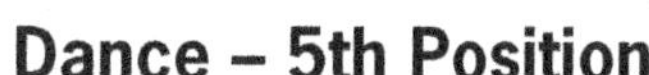

Dance – 5th Position

TRACK 6

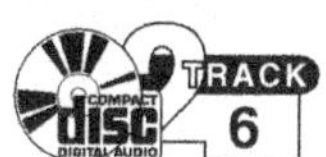

Moderately

W.B.

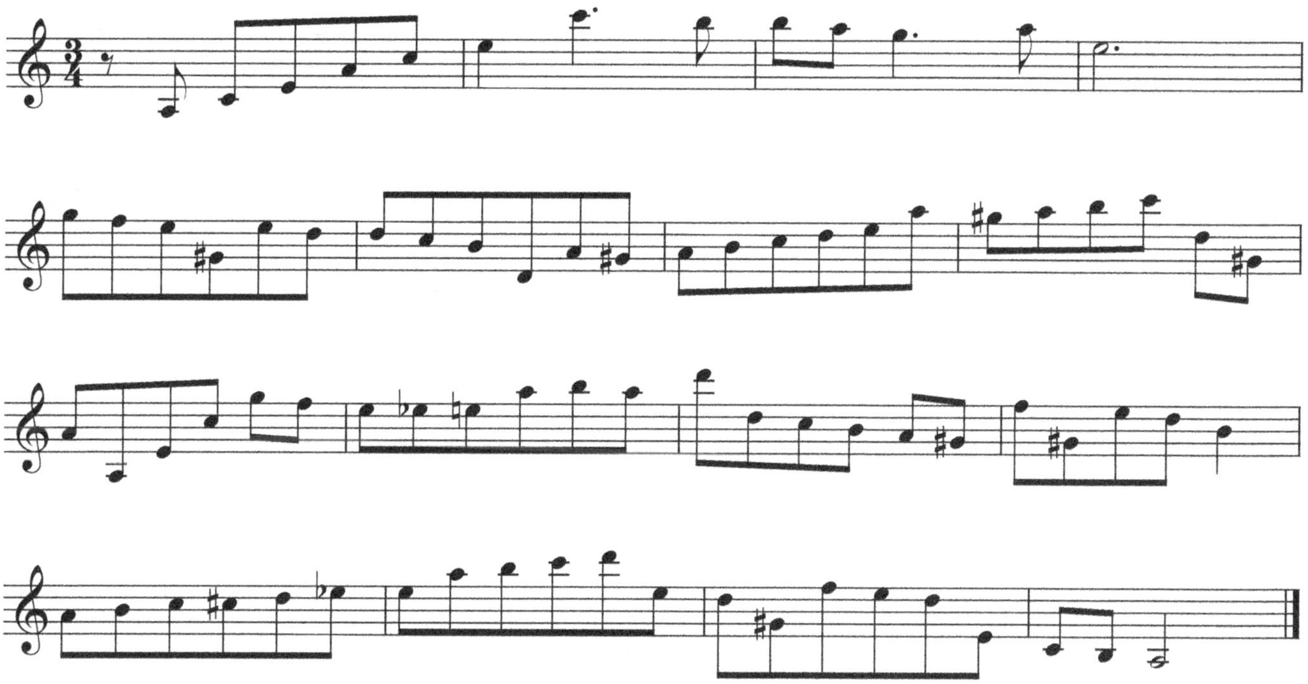

Silouette – 5th Position

TRACK 7

W.B.

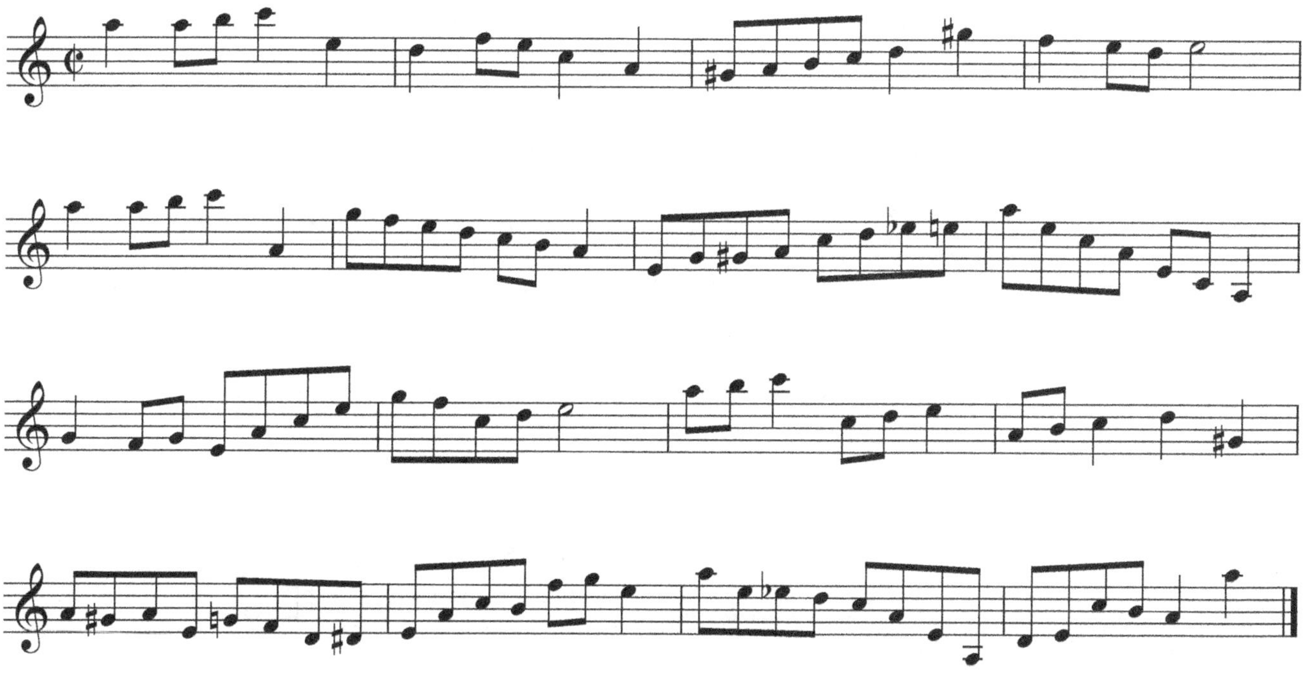

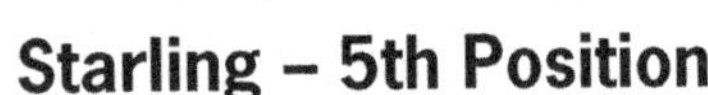

Starling – 5th Position

W.B.

Andante

Mirage – 5th Position

TRACK 9

W.B.

Allegro

Key of B♭ – 5th Position

B Flat Scale – 5th Position

B Flat Arpeggio – 5th Position

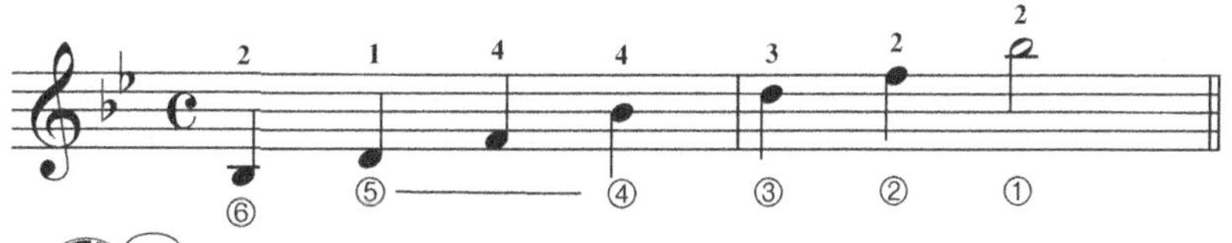

B♭ Scale Etude

TRACK 10

B♭ Studies – 5th Position

①

Song – 5th Position
TRACK 12
Allegro
W.B.
Exploration – 5th Position
TRACK 13
Slowly
W.B.

Etude – 5th Position

Allegro

Mel Bay

1 4 2 4 3 4

1 1

ritard

Minuetto

Guitar Duet
(Both parts in V Pos.)

I. Pleyel, Opus 48
Arr. by Mel Bay

D.C. al Fine
Two Triplet Etudes in the Fifth Position
TRACK 16
(Observe stroking.)
①
②
TRACK 17

DeSoto – 5th Position
TRACK 18
Allegro
W.B.
Dora's Waltz – 5th Position
TRACK 19
Moderately
W.B.

Key of E♭ – 5th Position

E Flat Scale – 5th Position

E Flat Arpeggio – 5th Position

Erin's Waltz – 5th Position

TRACK 20

W.B.

Cross Country – 5th Position

(1) 2

Snapshop – 5th Position

TRACK 22

Moderately

W.B.

4 2 4 2

Major Chord Etude #3
C F B♭ E♭ A♭ D♭ G♭
F♯ B E A D G C
The Notation of the Major Chords
C F B♭ E♭ A♭ D♭ G♭
F♯ B E A D G C
Poem
TRACK 23
Lento
Fibich
Arr. by Mel Bay
Cm E7 Am F G7 G7 C
D7 C E7 Am D7 G
C Am Dm D- Am Dm G7
Am Fm C
G7 C Am Fm C
Dm G7 C Am Fm
C Dm G7 C

The Trill

When a note alternates according to its value very rapidly with a tone or half tone above it, the effect produced is termed "the trill." This is best produced by picking the first or principal note and slurring the upper auxiliary note.

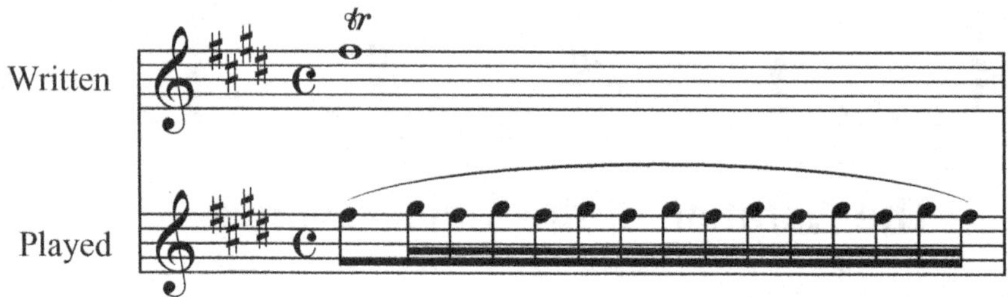

The Major Chord Inversions

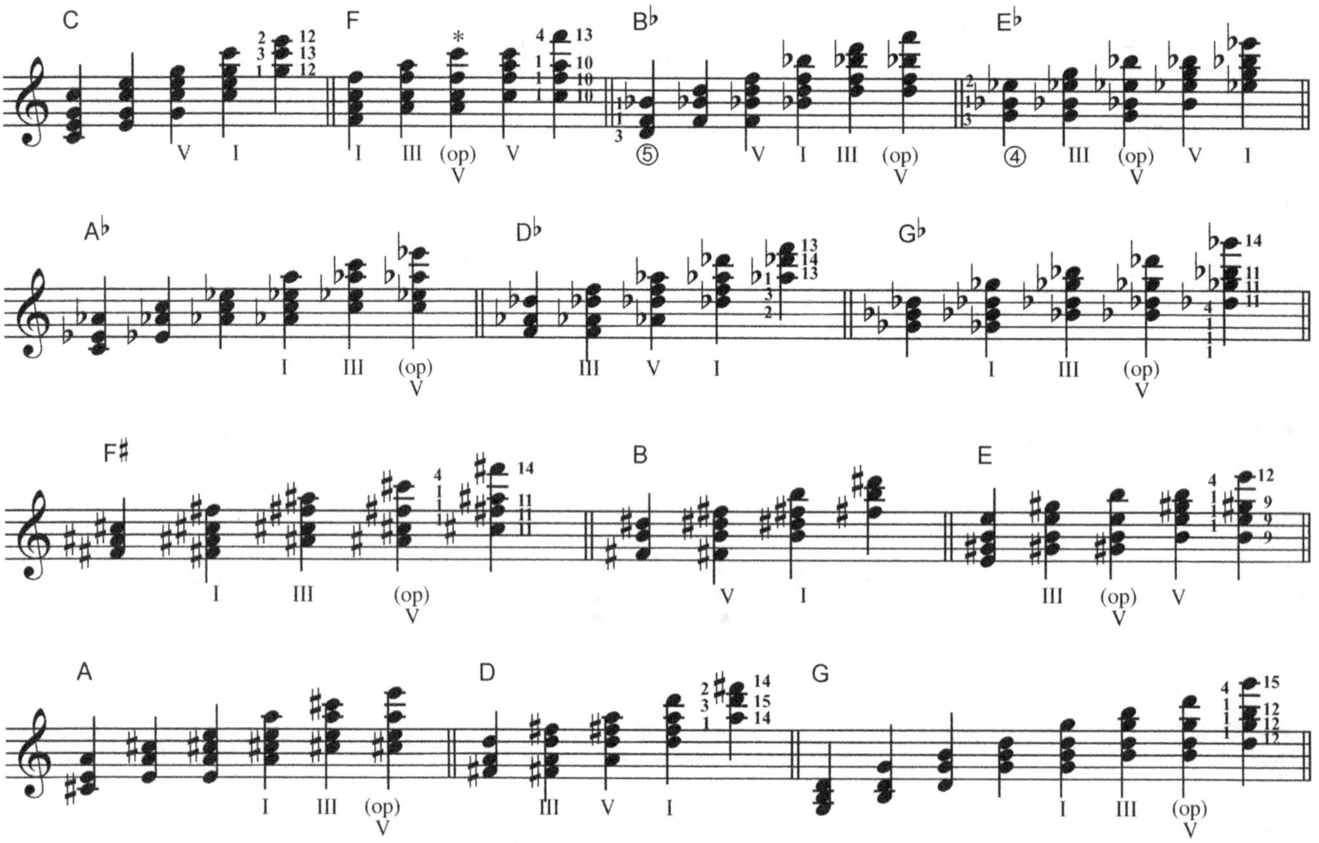

C — V I

F — I III (op) V V

B♭ — ⑤ V I III (op) V

E♭ — ④ III (op) V V I

A♭ — I III (op) V

D♭ — III V I

G♭ — I III (op) V

F♯ — I III (op) V

B — V I

E — III (op) V V

A — I III (op) V

D — III V I

G — I III (op) V

* In the higher positions where form V becomes difficult to finger, use the optional form V (op. V) as shown.

The Mordente

The mordente is a fragment of a trill. It is indicated by the sign 𝆗.

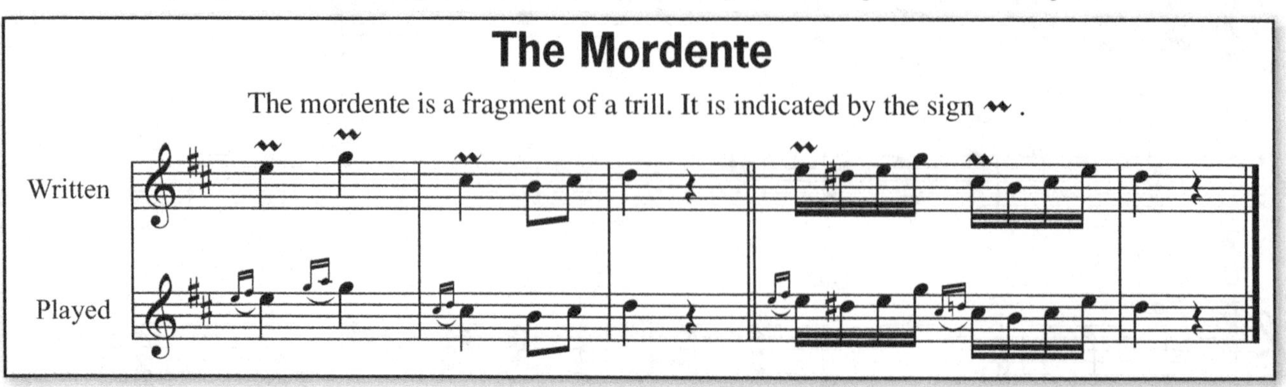

The Minor Chords

The major and minor chords have the same note-spelling, but the third of the minor chord is a half step lower. Example: C (C-E-G), Cm (C-E♭-G). The intervals of the minor chord are root, min. 3rd, perfect 5th.

The Minor Chord Forms

The minor chord forms are designated as I_m, III_m, and V_m (m = minor).

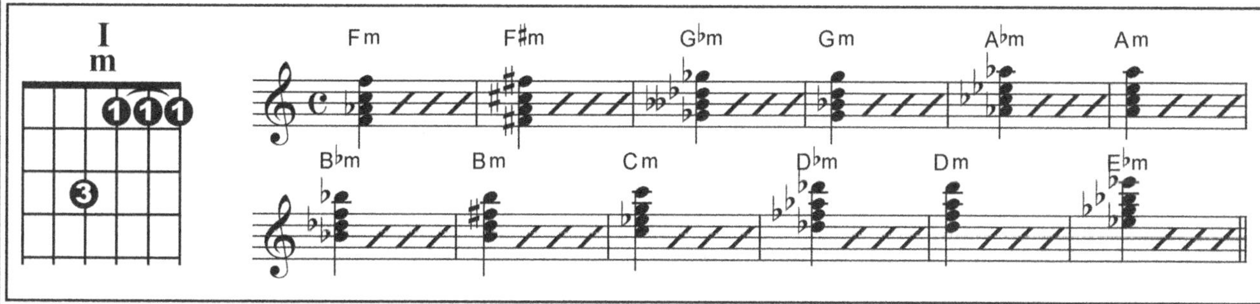

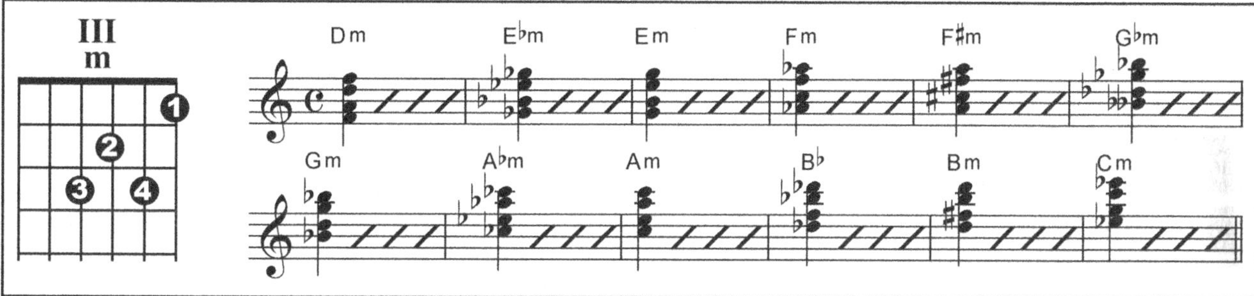

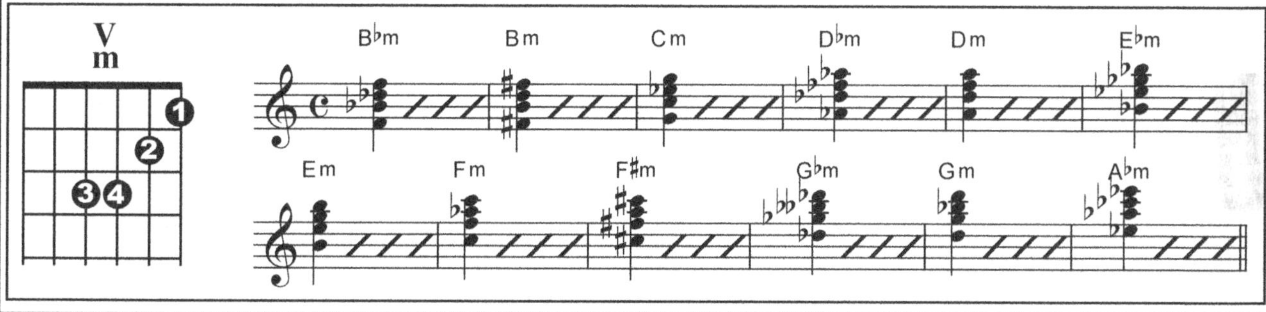

Minor Chord Etude #1

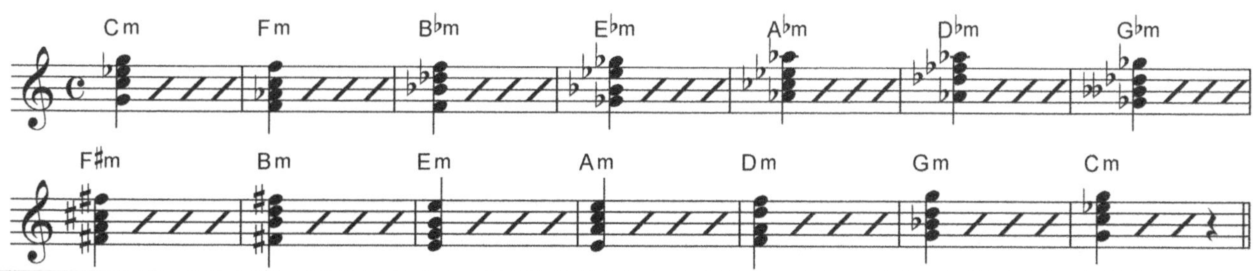

The Note-Spelling of the Major Chords

Cm (C-E♭-G)	Fm (F-A♭-C)	B♭m (B♭-D♭-F)	E♭m (E♭-G♭-B♭)	A♭m (A♭-C♭-E♭)
D♭m (D♭-F-A♭)	G♭m (G♭-B♭♭-D♭)	F♯m (F♯-A-C♯)	Bm (B-D-F♯)	Em (E-G-B)
	Am (A-C-E)	Dm (D-F-A)	Gm (G-B♭-D)	

The Seventh Position

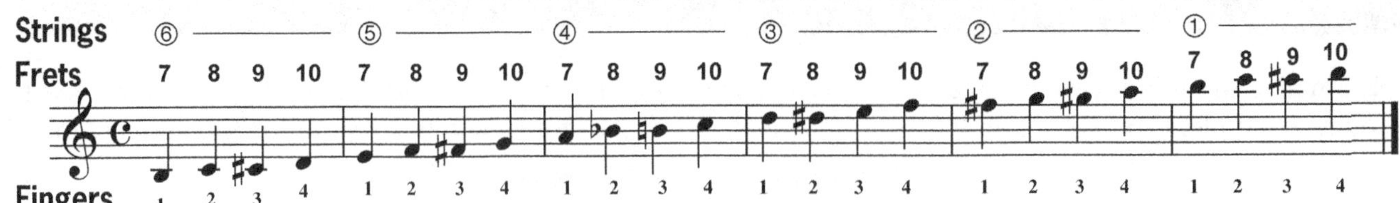

C Scale – 7th Position

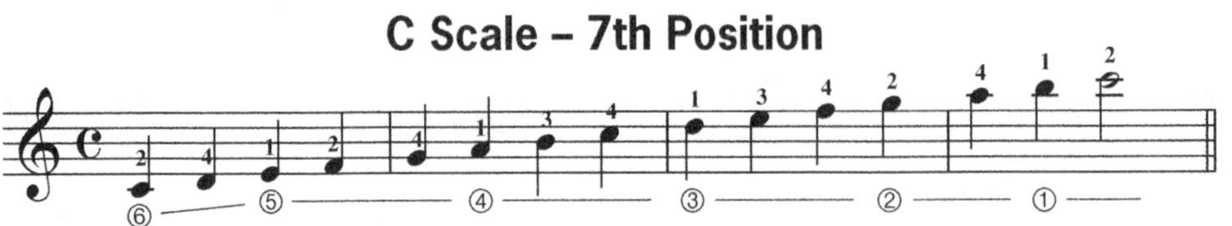

C Arpeggio – 7th Position

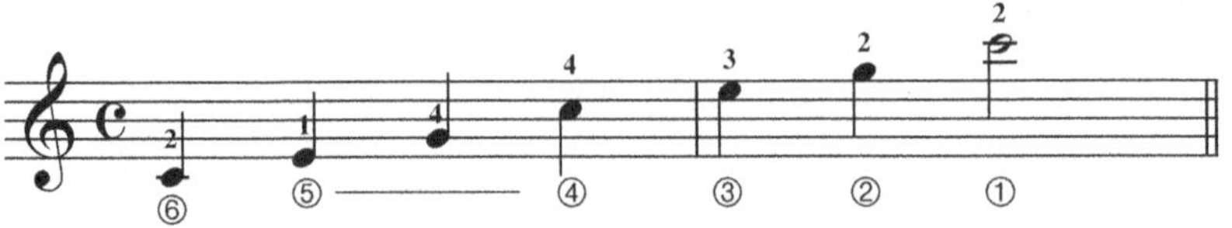

Seventh-Position Etude

TRACK 24

Fast

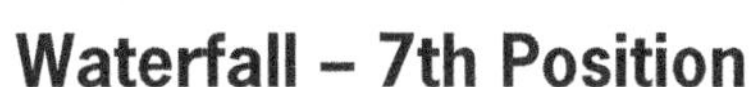

Waterfall – 7th Position

TRACK 25

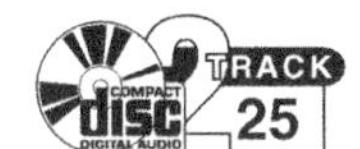

Allegro

W.B.

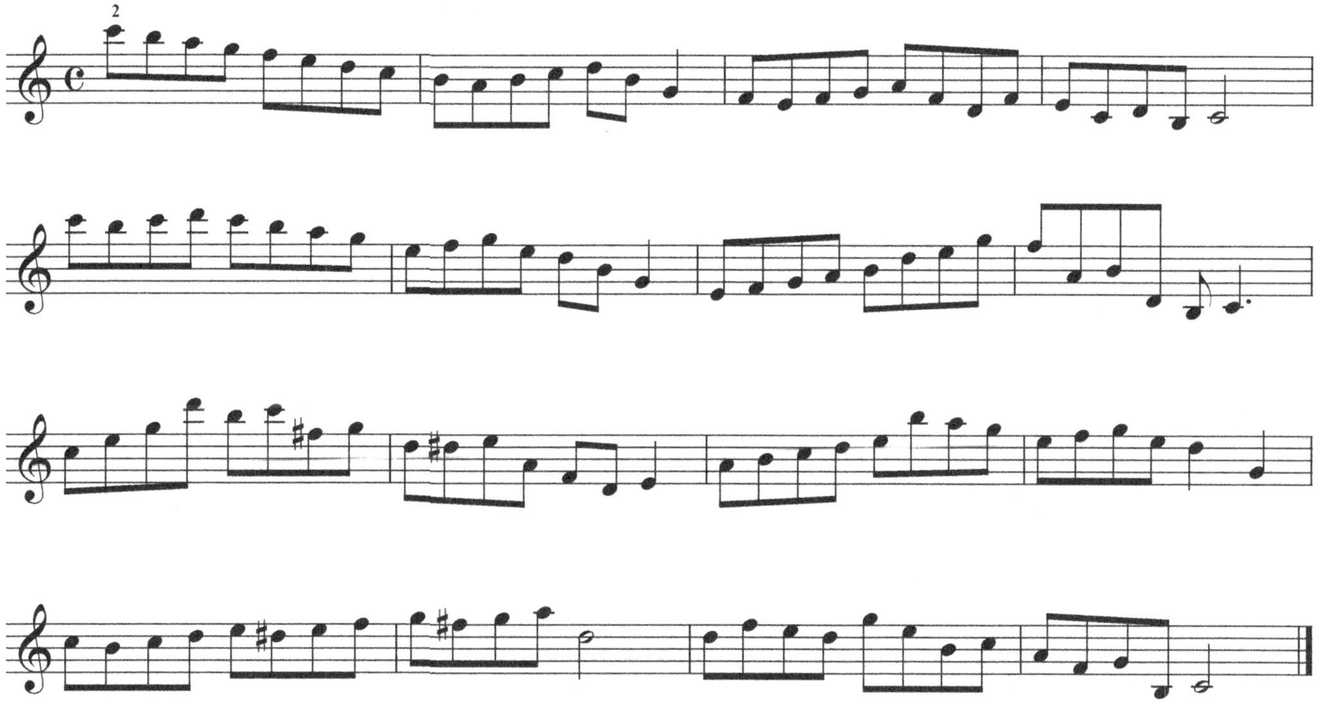

Joplin – 7th Position

TRACK 26

Moderately

W.B.

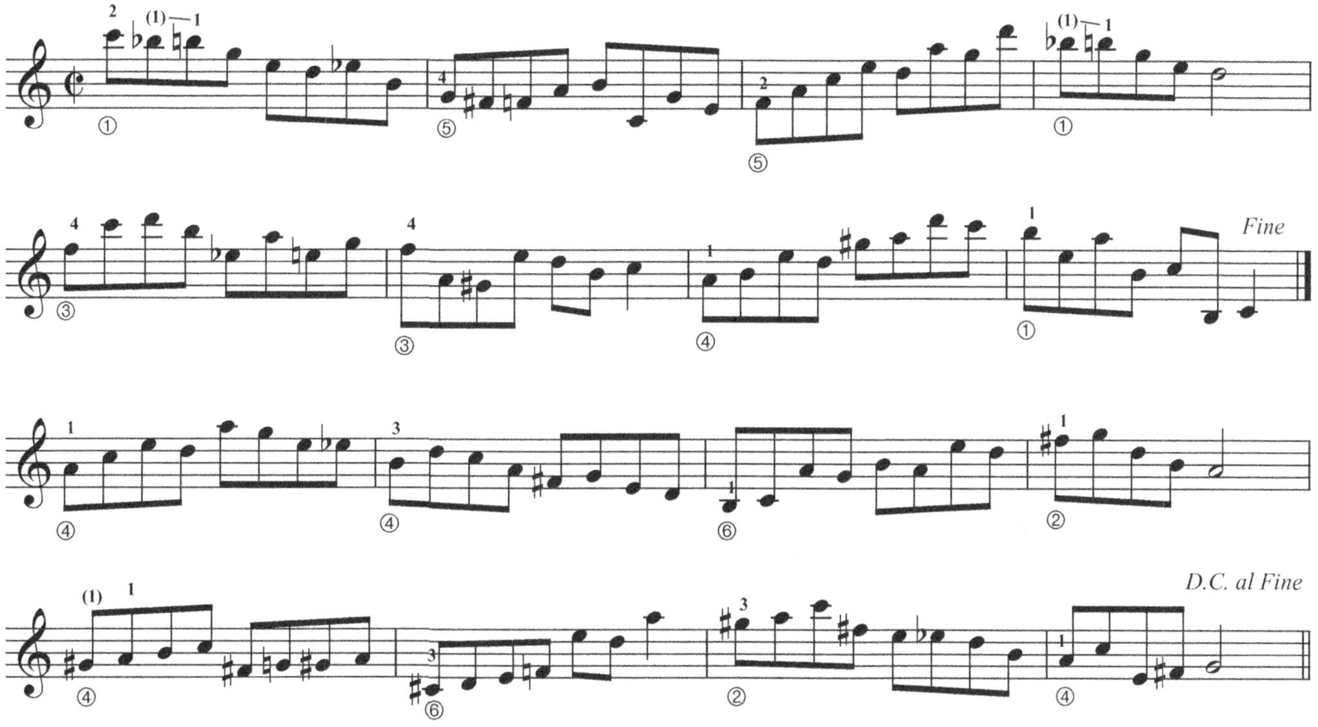

Fine
D.C. al Fine

Kreutzer's Etude – 7th Position

Rudolphe Kreutzer

Allegro moderato

Key of G – 7th Position

Breathe on Me, Breath of God
TRACK 30
Hymn
W.B.
Slowly
G C Cm G
(hold chord)
Am A7 D G D7 G
Em Am G D7 A° G
Lucky Seven – 7th Position
TRACK 31
Guitar Solo
VII Pos.
Fine
rit.
D.S. al Fine

Minor Chord Etude #2

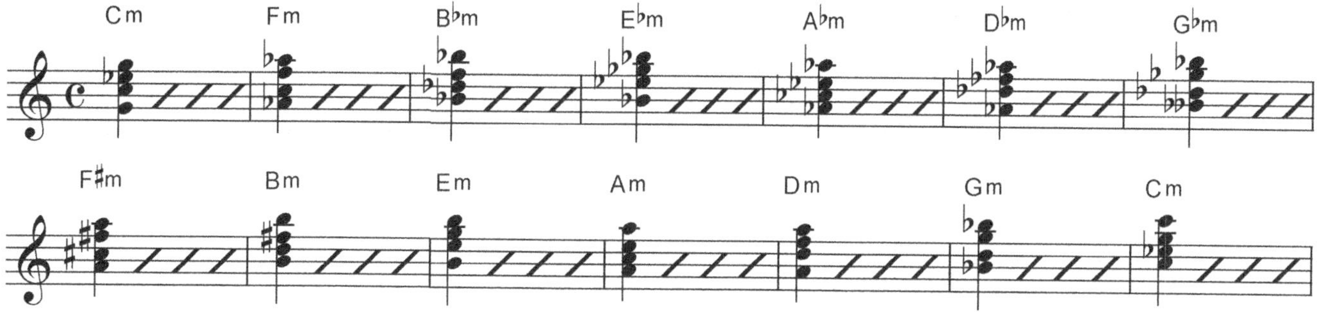

Minor Chord Etude #3

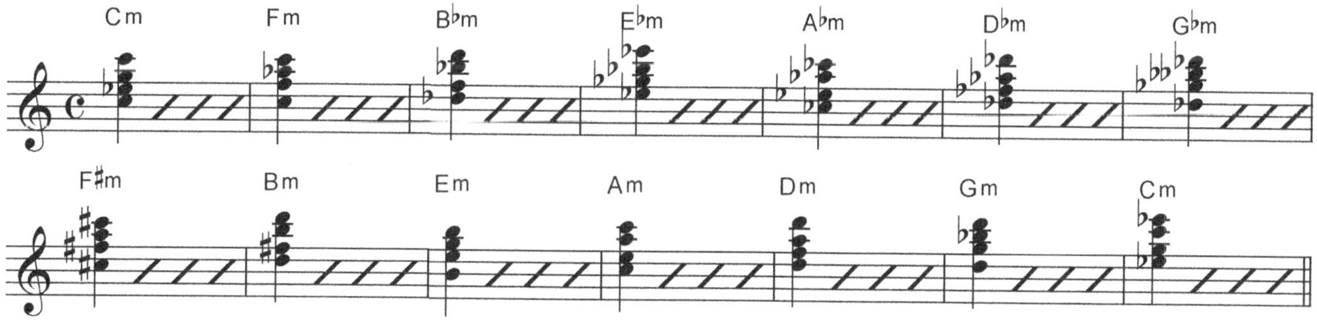

The Minor Chord Inversions

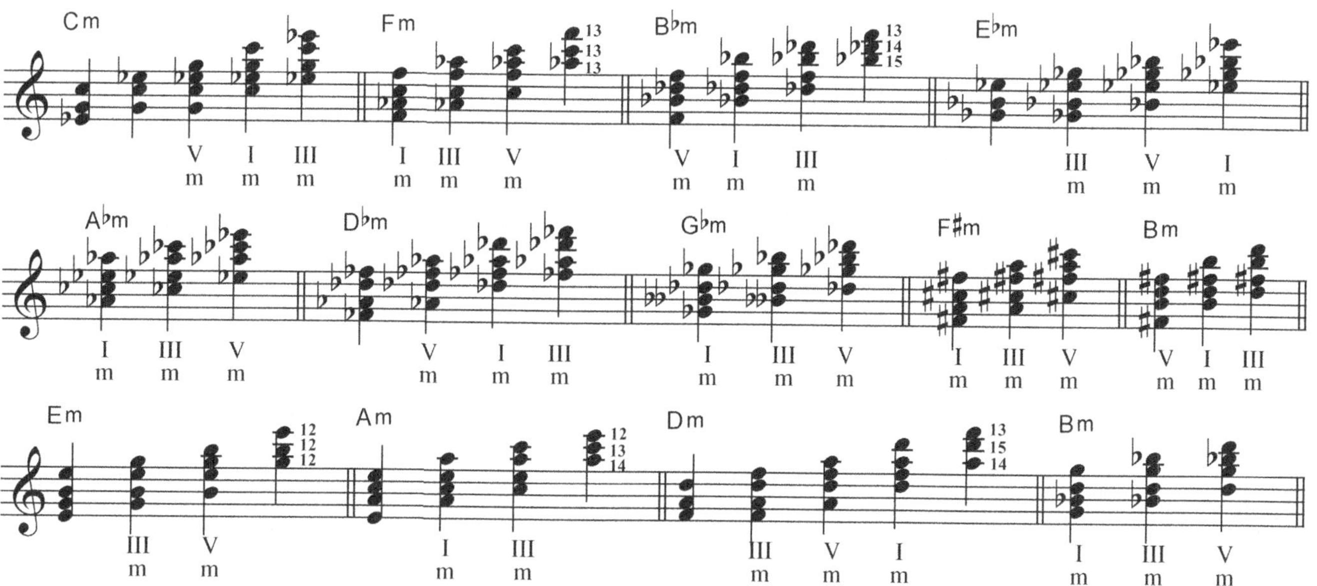

*By playing open, the student will be in the first position for minor portion.

G Major
VII Pos.

Scale Study – 7th Position

TRACK 33

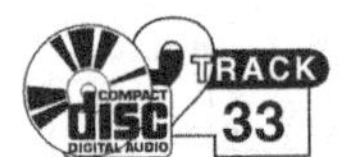

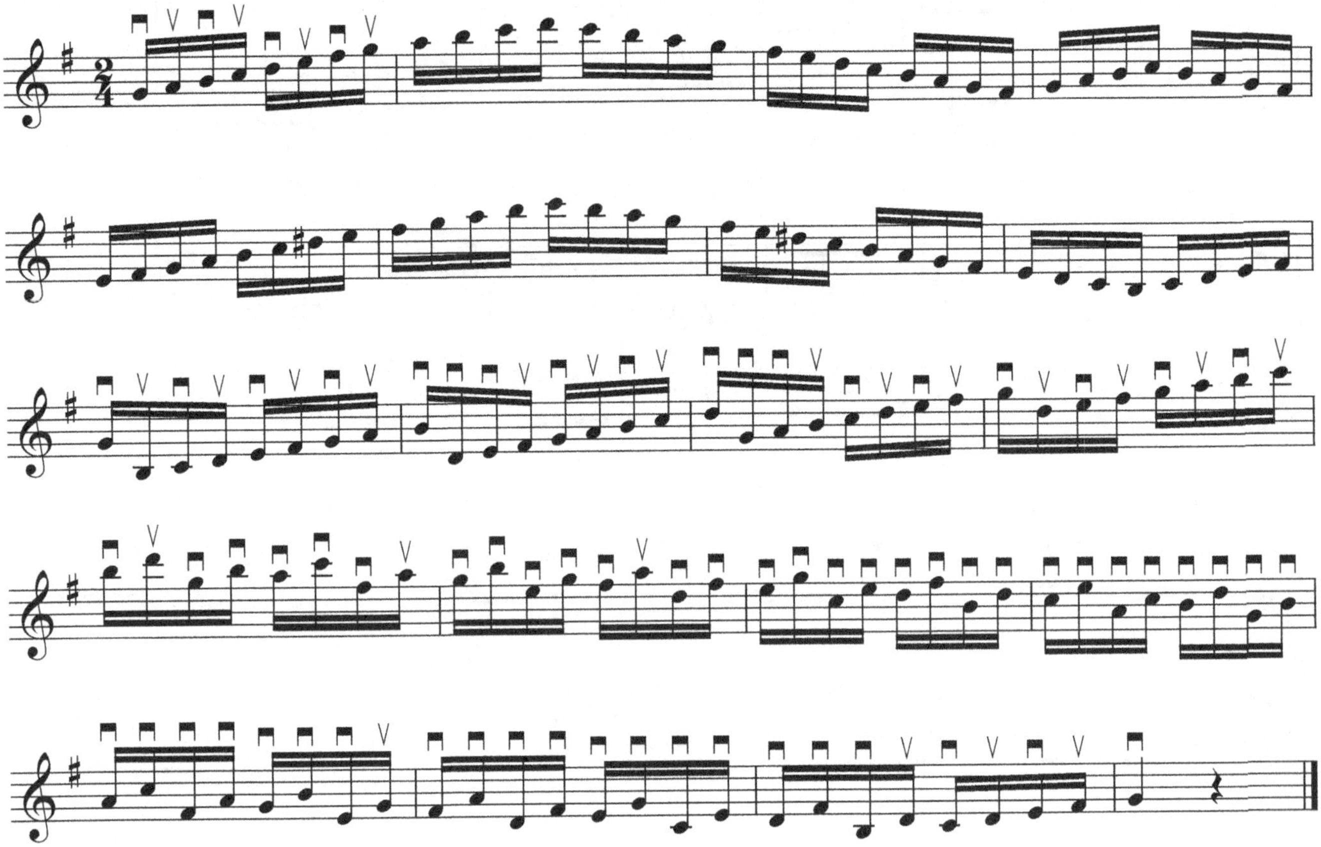

Gardenia – 7th Position

TRACK 34

Moderately

W.B.

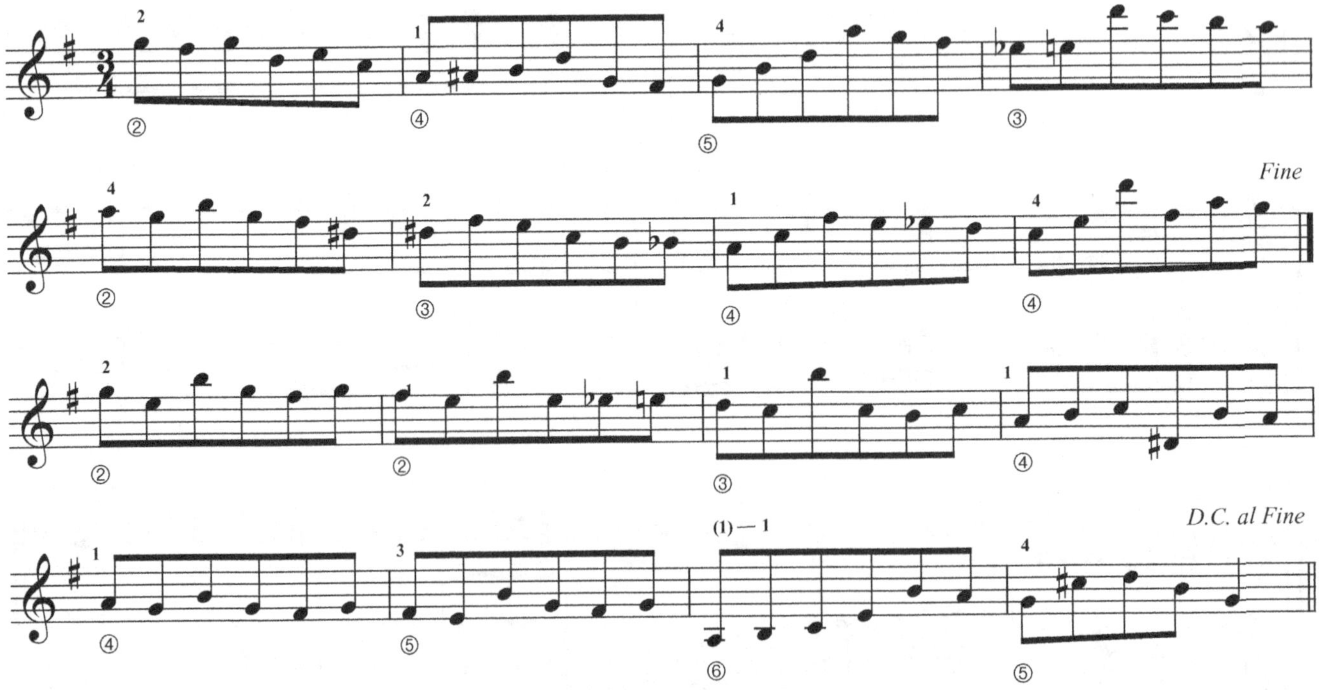

Fine
D.C. al Fine

The Dominant Seventh Chord

The intervals of the dominant seventh chord are root, major 3rd, perfect 5th, and minor 7th. The dominant seventh in the fundamental or root position consists of a major 3rd, minor 3rd, and a minor 3rd (see construction below).

The dominant seventh chord is named after the dominant (V) degree of the scale. The three principal chords in any major or minor key are the tonic, sub-dominant, and dominant seventh chords.

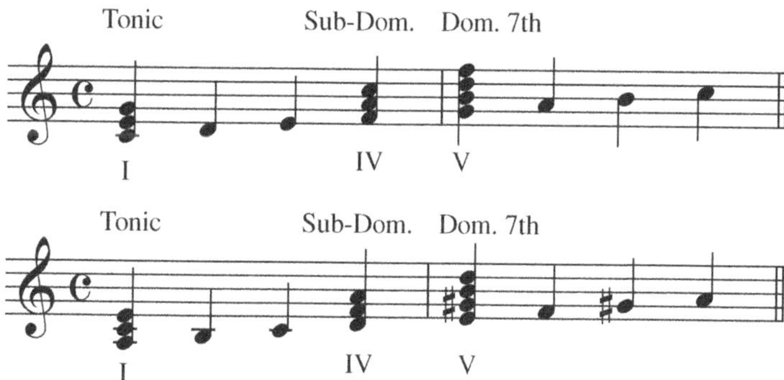

In this method, the student will be shown how the above chords are applied in the harmonizing and accompaniment of melodies with ear-training exercises.

The construction of a dominant seventh chord is best accomplished by taking the 1st, 3rd, 5th, and **lowered 7th** of any **major scale.**

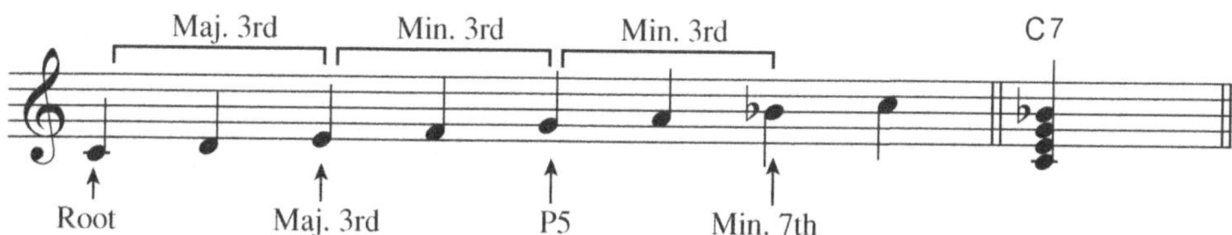

The student should write out all major scales, construct the dominant seventh chords by the above method and memorize the note-spelling of the chords.

The Notation of the Dominant Seventh Chord

Gypsy Rondo – 7th Pos.
TRACK
35
Joseph Haydn
Arr. by Mel Bay
Presto
I
II
G D7 G D7
G
Am E7 Am A7
D7
G
Am
Am7 D7
G
G D7 G D7
G
E7 Am A7
D7
G
Am
Am7 D7
G
Em B7 Em A7
D A7 D
G A7
D
D G
D
D G
D

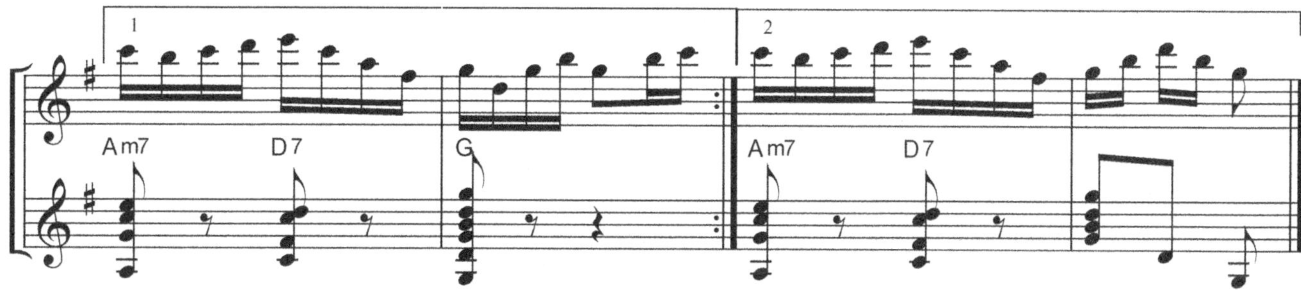

The following studies should be played by placing the first finger over the 1st, 2nd, and 3rd strings at the seventh fret. Hold the bar while playing the following passages.

The above passage can be found in the 1st, 2nd, 9th, 10th, 27th, and 28th measures of "Gypsy Rondo."

The following passages can be found in the 21st, 22nd, 23rd, and 24th measures of "Gypsy Rondo." Bar the seventh fret as shown above.

The following passages can be found in the 26th and 27th measures of the same selection and should be played by barring the seventh fret on the first three strings.

After carefully mastering the above passages, play "Gypsy Rondo," keeping the seventh fret barred throughout and lifting the bar only where necessary.

The Notation of the Major and Minor Chords

Memorize but do not play.

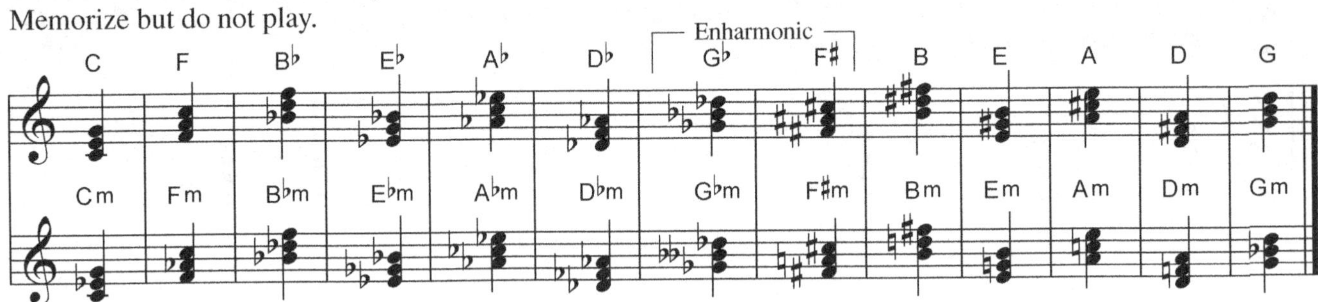

Major to Tonic Minor Etude

Major to Relative Minor Etude

The relative minor chord is built upon the sixth degree of the major scale.

Major to Tonic Minor Etude

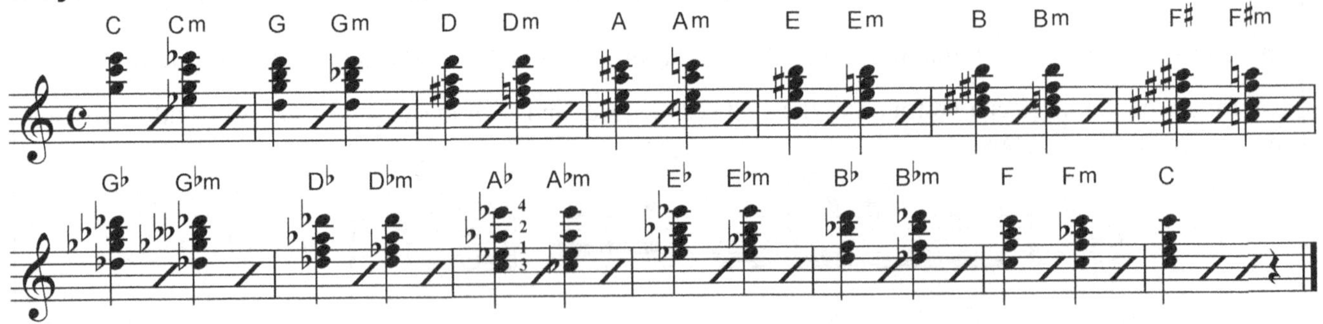

Major to Relative Minor Etude

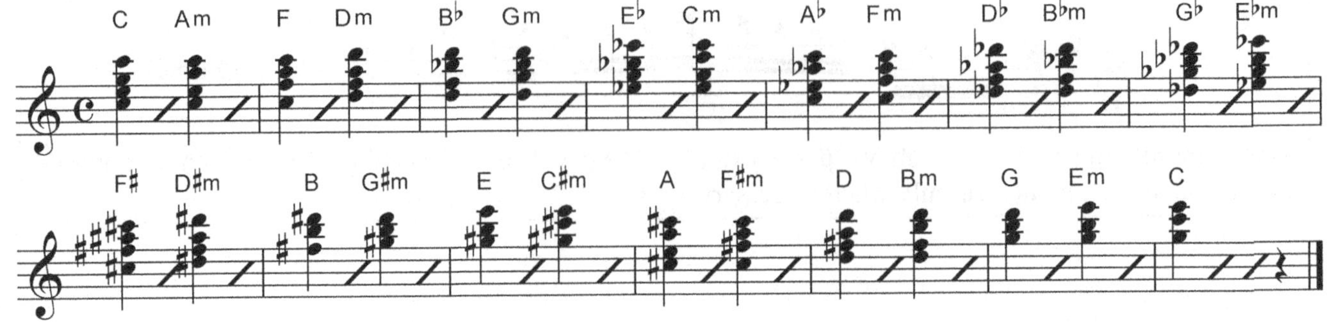

The Seventh Chords

The seventh chord forms will be numbered I7, III7, V7, AND VII7, corresponding to the chord intervals found on the first string. The note played on the first string is often referred to as the "top note" of the chord.

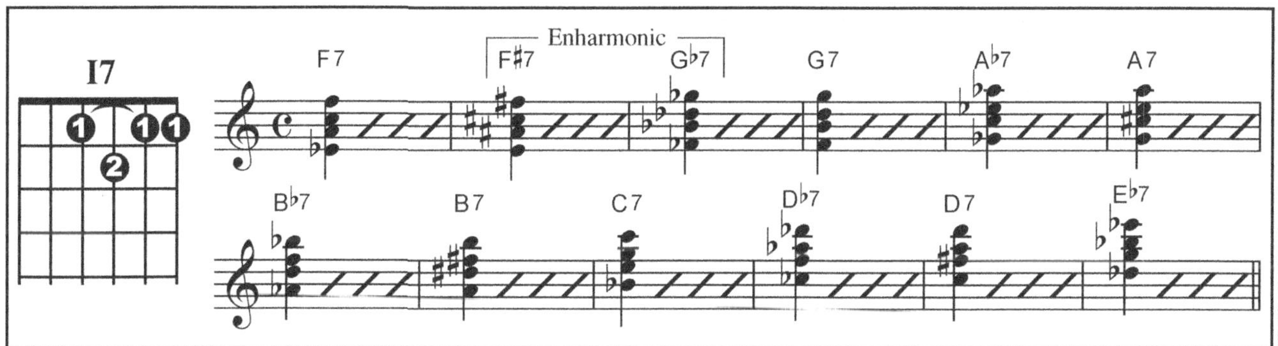

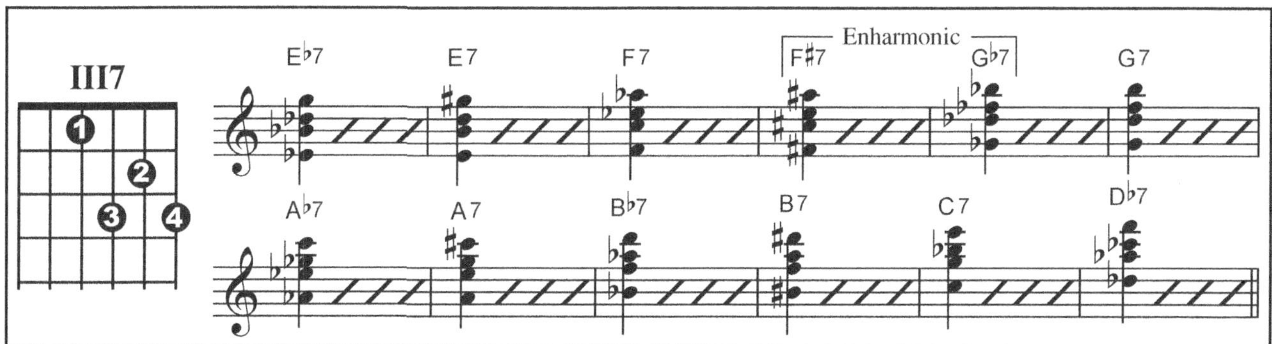

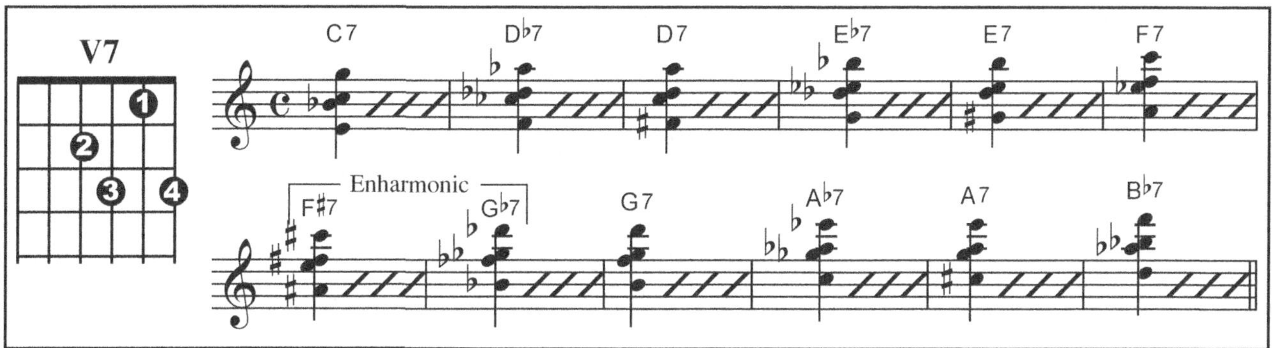

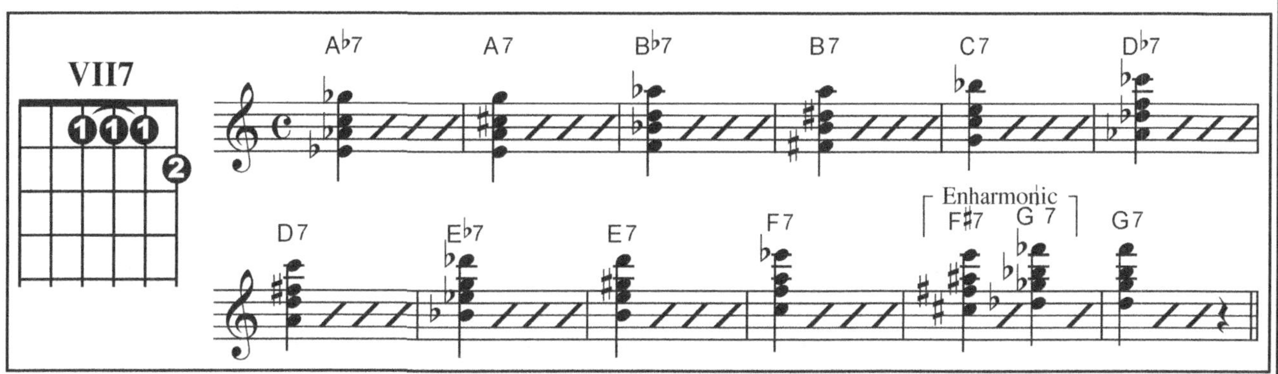

Key of Em – 7th Position

E Minor Scale / Harmonic Mode – 7th Position

E Minor Arpeggio – 7th Position

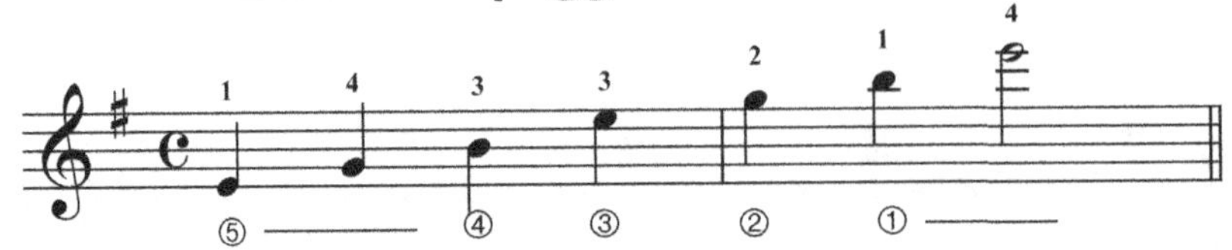

Portrait – 7th Position

Andante

W.B.

Discovery – 7th Position

Andante

W.B.

Dawn– 7th Position

TRACK 38

Moderately

W.B.

Key of Bm – 7th Position

B Minor Scale / Harmonic Mode – 7th Position

B Minor Arpeggio – 7th Position

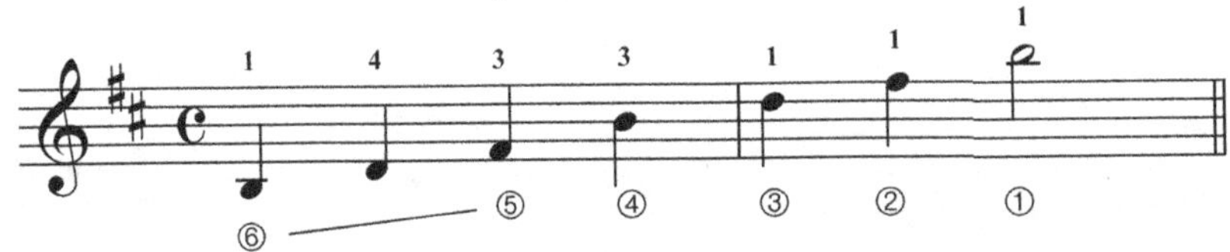

Passage – 7th Position

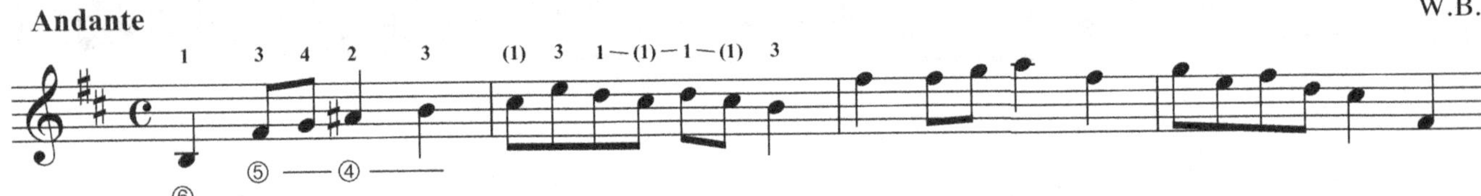

Misty Night – 7th Position

Key of F – 7th Position

F Scale – 7th Position

F Arpeggio – 7th Position

Vista – 7th Position

TRACK 42

Andante

W.B.

Fine

D.C. al Fine

Workout– 7th Position

Moderately

W.B.

2

⑤

Glasgow– 7th Position

TRACK 44

Moderately

W.B.

2 1 4 2 1 4

⑤ ④

Key of Dm – 7th Position

D Minor Scale / Harmonic Mode – 7th Position

D Minor Arpeggio – 7th Position

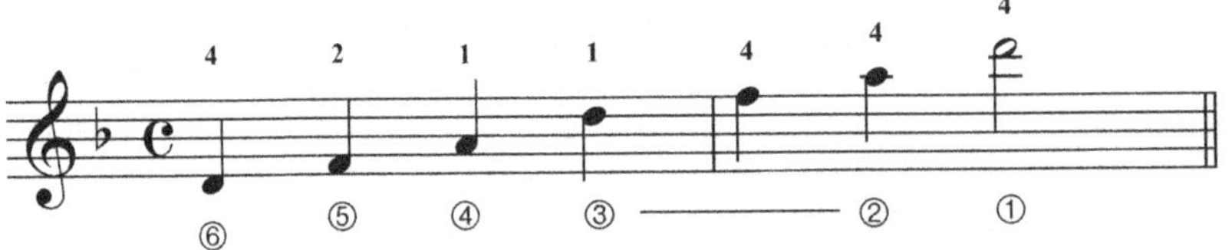

Sunset – 7th Position

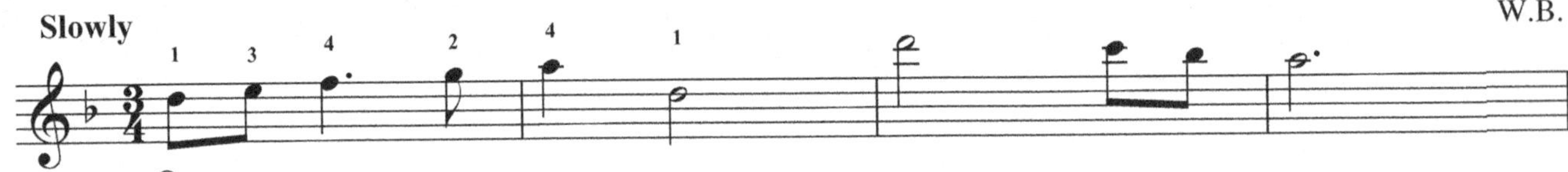

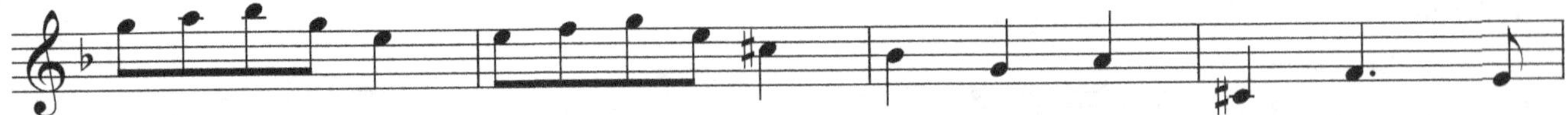

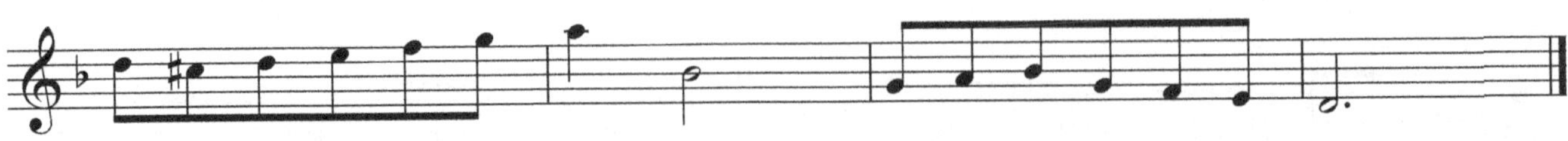

Autumn – 7th Position

Key of D – 7th Position

D Scale – 7th Position

D Arpeggio – 7th Position

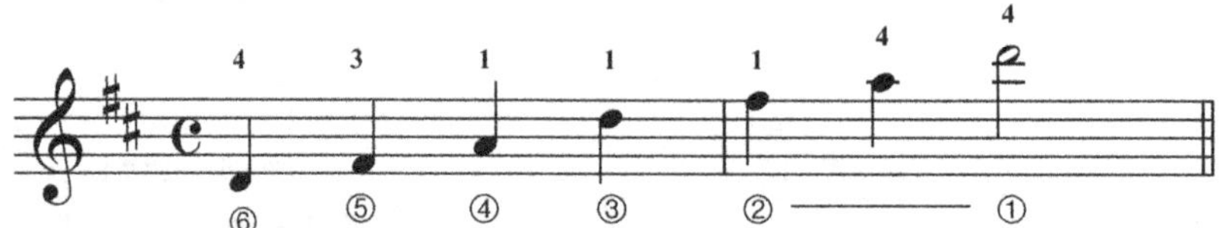

Cruising – 7th Position

TRACK 48

Moderately

W.B.

Muse – 7th Position

TRACK 49

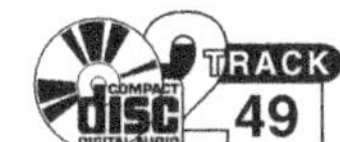

Allegro

W.B.

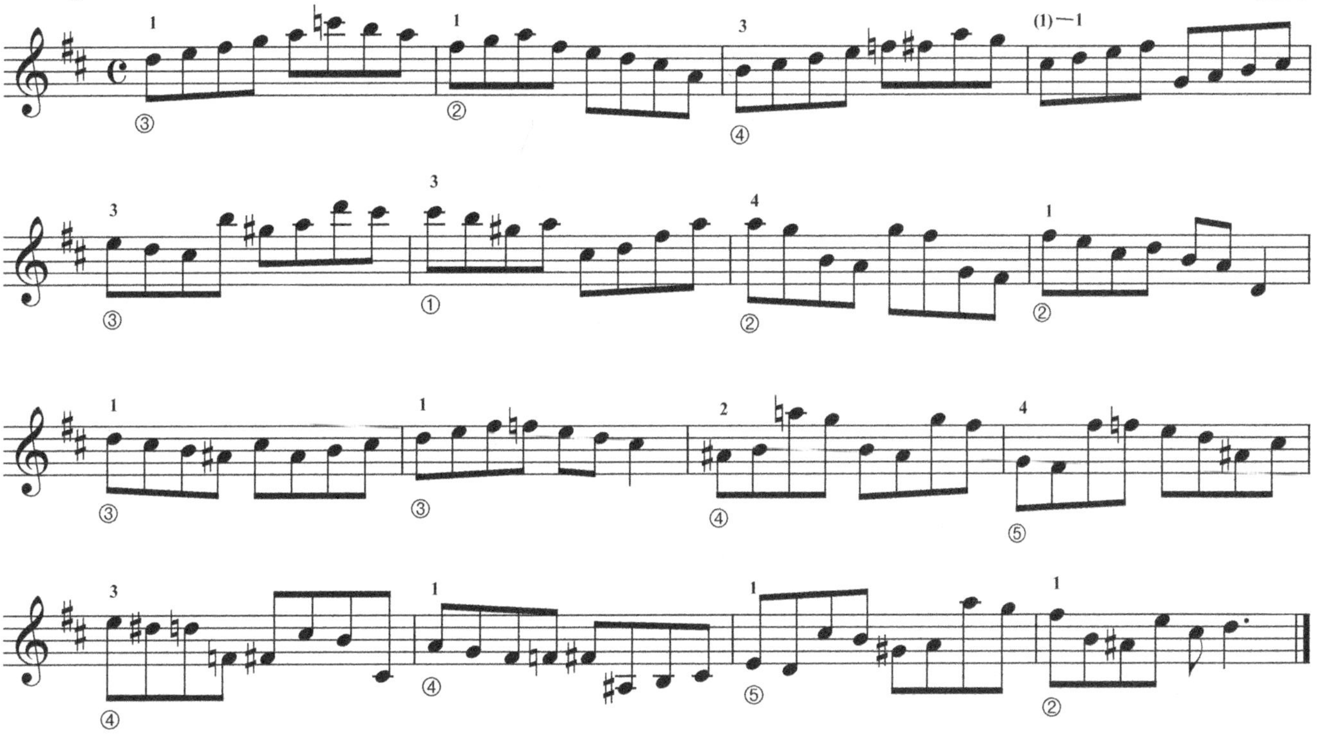

Snowfall – 7th Position

TRACK 50

Moderately

W.B.

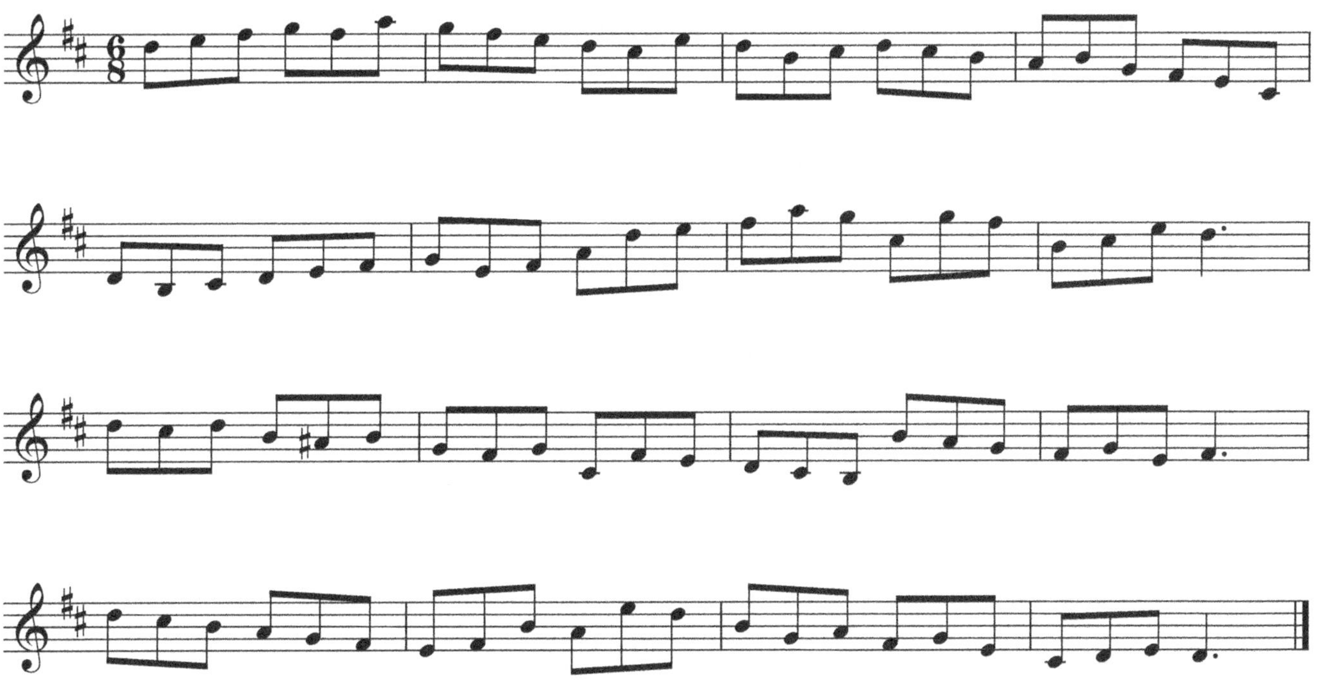

Key of Gm – 7th Position

G Minor Scale / Harmonic Mode – 7th Position

G Minor Arpeggio – 7th Position

Panorama – 7th Position

Natasha – 7th Position

Slowly

W.B.

Farewell – 7th Position

TRACK 53

Allegro

W.B.

The Ninth Position

Key of A – 9th Position

A Scale – 9th Position

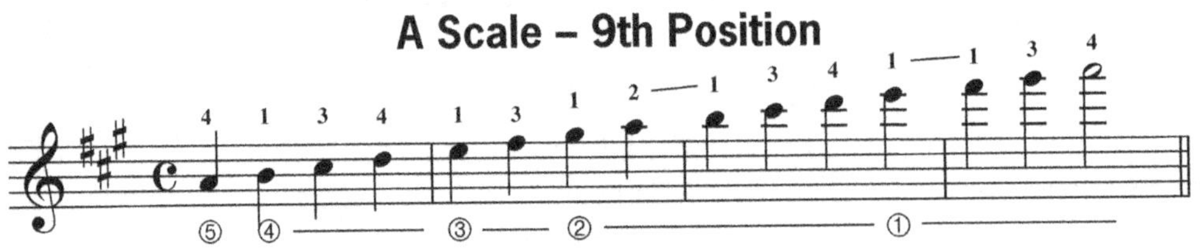

A Arpeggio – 9th Position

Ninth-Position Etude #1

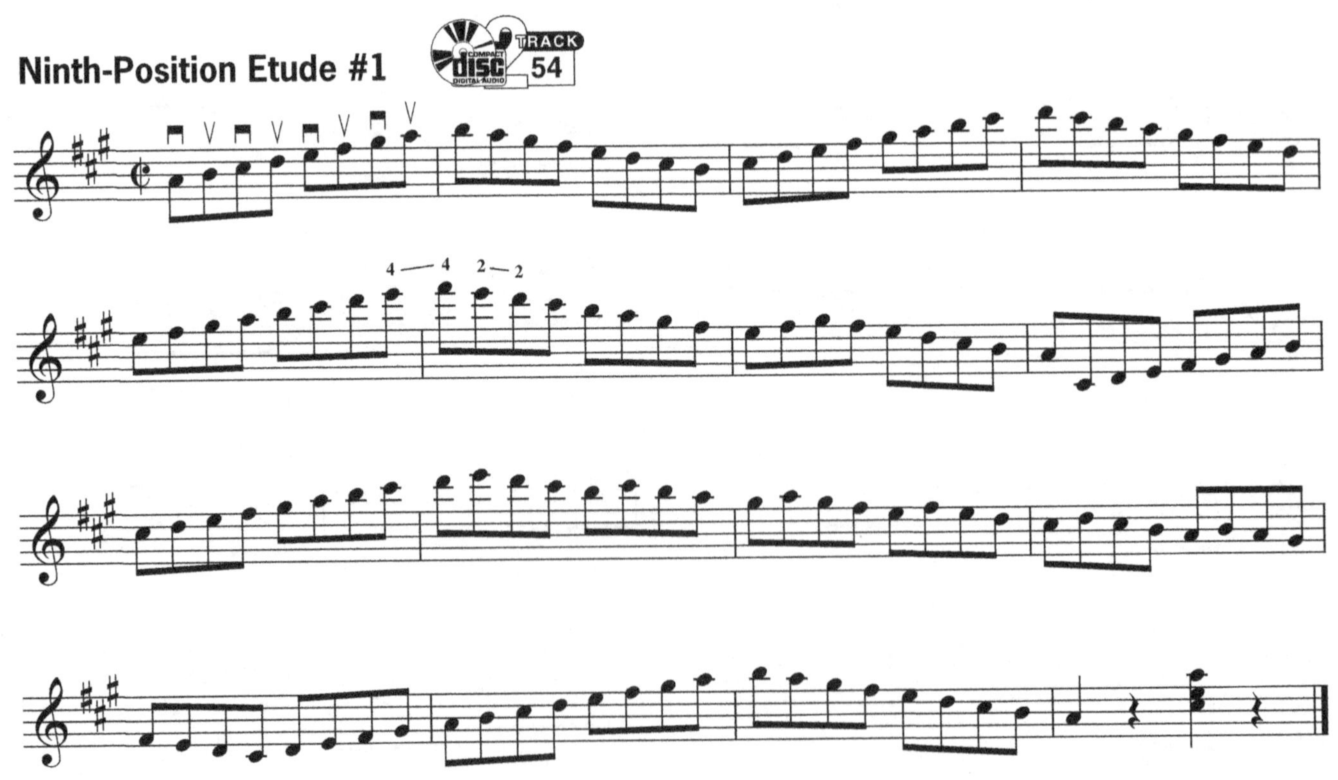

Ninth-Position Etude #2

The Ninth Inning – 9th Position

TRACK 56

Guitar Solo

Allegro

Carcassi-Bay

rit.

Maze – 9th Position

Seventh-Chord Etude #1

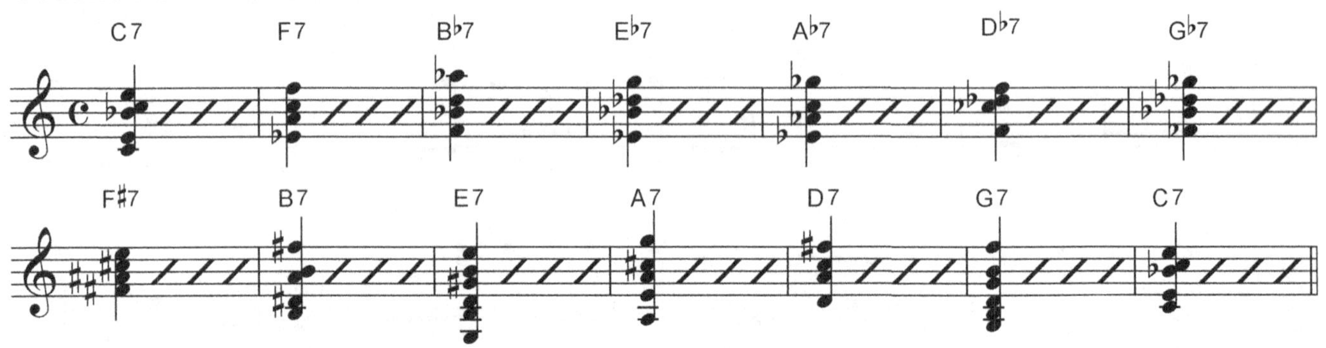

Seventh-Chord Etude #2

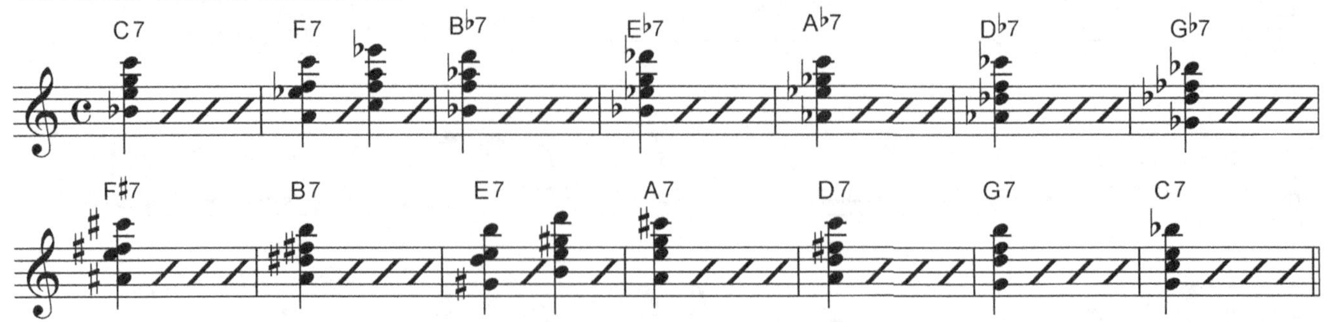

Seventh-Chord Etude #3

Susan Lynn – Multiple Positions

The Golden Wedding (La Cinquantaine)
TRACK 59
Gabriel-Marie
Arr. by Mel Bay
Moderato
Fine
Key of A Major
D.S. al Fine

Inversions
C7
V7 VII7 I7 III7
F7
I7 III7 V7 VII7
B♭7
Op VII7 I7 III7 V7
E♭7
III7 V7 VII7 I7
A♭7
D♭7
V7 VII7 I7 III7
G♭7
I7 III7 V7 VII7
F♯7
I7 III7 V7 VII7
B7
VII7 I7 III7 V7
E7
III7 V7 VII7
A7
VII7 I7 III7 V7
D7
V7 VII7 I7 III7
G7
I7 III7 V7 VII7
Carcassi's Etude (A Major)
TRACK 60
Guitar Solo
Andantino
Carcassi
V Pos
II Pos
III Pos
VII Pos
IV Pos
IX Pos
cresc.
rall.

Norwegian Dance

Guitar Duet

Grieg, Opus 35
Arr. by Mel Bay

Key of A Minor

Allegretto

Excursion (A Position Review)

Guitar Solo (Roman numeral = position)

Carcassi-Bay

VII
VII
VII
V
rallentando
a tempo
IV
V
II
IX
VII
V
IV
IX

VII
V
IV
f
cresc.
V
VII
V
cresc.
III
III
f
VII

Modulation One

Modulation Two

Mel Bay

You are now ready to proceed with Grade 5!

Made in the USA
Middletown, DE
30 December 2023